THE ULTIMATE RESOURCE FOR SOFTWARE PROJECT MANAGERS

100 Email Templates for Every Project Scenario

Rahul Parmar

CONTENTS

OVERCOMING COMMUNICATION CHALLENGES: JOHN'S STORY

Meet John, a software project manager who had been in the industry for over a decade. He had worked on numerous projects throughout his career, some of which had been a resounding success, while others had failed miserably. But no matter the outcome, one thing was certain: communication played a critical role in determining the success or failure of a project.

As John worked on various projects, he began to notice that crafting the right emails for each situation was a time-consuming and often frustrating task. He would spend hours drafting and revising emails, trying to strike the right tone and convey the right message, only to end up feeling unsure about whether he had communicated effectively.

It was during one particularly challenging project that John realized he needed a better solution. The project was complex, involving multiple stakeholders with competing priorities, and John struggled to keep everyone on the same page. He found himself constantly sending and receiving emails, trying to clarify requirements, update stakeholders on progress, and manage expectations. He spent so much time on email communication that he began to neglect other important aspects of the project.

That's when John realized the value of having a set of email templates that he could rely on in various project scenarios. With a template, he could quickly draft an email and customize it to suit the situation, without having to start from scratch each time. He could ensure that he conveyed the right message in a clear and concise way, without wasting time on revisions and editing.

The story of John is not unique. As a software project manager, you too may have faced communication challenges that have impeded the success of your projects. With "100+ Email Templates for Software Project Managers," you can streamline your communication process, save time, and achieve better outcomes for your projects. Let this book be your guide to success, and don't let communication challenges hold you back any longer.

MASTERING EMAIL COMMUNICATION: BEST PRACTICES AND PITFALLS TO AVOID

Effective communication is critical to the success of any software project, and emails are a key component of communication in project management. However, crafting effective emails can be a challenging task, especially in the fast-paced environment of software development. To help software project managers overcome these challenges, this section will share some best practices for effective communication through emails and examples of what to avoid in project communication.

Keep it Clear and Concise

The first rule of effective email communication is to keep it clear and concise. Avoid using technical jargon or acronyms that the recipient may not understand. Keep your sentences short and to the point, and use bullet points to highlight key information. This approach will help ensure that the recipient understands the message you are trying to convey, even if they are not a technical expert.

Use the Right Tone

The tone of your email is just as important as the content. You want to strike a tone that is professional, yet friendly and approachable. Avoid using language that is too formal or too casual, and be mindful of the recipient's cultural background. Always be polite and respectful, even if you disagree with the recipient.

Be Mindful of Timing

Timing is everything when it comes to email communication. Avoid sending emails late at night or early in the morning, as this can give the impression that you are working around the clock and may lead to burnout. Similarly, avoid sending emails on weekends or holidays unless it is absolutely necessary. Always be mindful of the recipient's time zone and work schedule.

Use Descriptive Subject Lines

Your subject line should be descriptive and concise, and should accurately reflect the content of the email. This will help the recipient prioritize their emails and ensure that they do not miss anything important.

Examples of What to Avoid in Project Communication:

Rambling Emails

Avoid emails that are too long and rambling. These emails can be overwhelming for the recipient and may cause them to lose interest in the message.

Negativity

Avoid using negative language or tone in your emails. This can be demotivating for the recipient and may harm the relationship between the sender and the recipient.

Spelling and Grammar Errors

Spelling and grammar errors can make the sender appear unprofessional and careless. Always proofread your emails before sending them.

Vague Requests

Avoid making vague requests in your emails. Always be specific about what you need from the recipient and provide clear instructions.

By following these best practices and avoiding common pitfalls in project communication, software project managers can improve their email communication and achieve better outcomes for their projects. The templates provided in this book are based on these best practices, and can help software project managers save time and communicate more effectively with their team members, clients, and stakeholders.

CRAFTING CUSTOMIZED EMAILS: TIPS FOR TAILORING TEMPLATES TO SUIT DIFFERENT SITUATIONS

While having email templates is a great starting point, customizing them for different situations is equally important for effective communication in software project management. In this section, we will provide tips for customizing the email templates to suit different situations and achieve the desired outcome.

Understand Your Audience

The first step in customizing your email templates is to understand your audience. Who are you communicating with? What is their background? What are their goals? By understanding your audience, you can tailor your language, tone, and content to match their needs and expectations.

Customize the Tone

The tone of your email should match the recipient and the situation. If you are communicating with a client, for example, you may want to use a more formal tone. If you are communicating with a team member, a more casual tone may be appropriate. You can also adjust the tone based on the urgency and importance of the message.

Personalize the Content

Personalizing the content of your email can help build a stronger relationship with the recipient. Use their name, reference previous conversations or interactions, and show that you understand their needs and concerns. This approach will help the recipient feel valued and understood.

Use the Right Language

Using the right language is critical for effective communication. Avoid technical jargon or acronyms that the recipient may not understand, and use plain language whenever possible. Use active voice and avoid passive voice, as it can make the message sound impersonal.

Tailor the Format

The format of your email can also be customized to suit different situations. For example, if you are communicating with a client, you may want to include a professional-looking signature with your contact information. If you are communicating with a team member, you may want to use bullet points to highlight key information.

By customizing your email templates using these tips, you can improve the effectiveness of your communication and achieve better outcomes for your projects. The templates provided in this book can be easily customized using these tips to suit your specific situation, making communication easier, faster, and more efficient.

EMAIL 1: PROVIDING FEEDBACK TO DEVELOPERS FOR CODE REVIEW

As a software project manager, providing feedback to developers is critical to ensuring that the project meets the highest standards of code quality and development efficiency. By taking the time to provide constructive feedback, you can help developers identify areas for improvement and optimize code performance. This can ultimately lead to a more streamlined development process, shorter project timelines, and higher-quality code. In this sample email, you'll learn how to provide effective feedback to developers after a code review, including the importance of recognizing their hard work, identifying areas for improvement, and explaining the long-term benefits of making changes. By following the tips provided in this email, you can become a more effective communicator and drive success in your software projects.

Sample Email:

Subject Line: Code Review Feedback on [Project Name]

Dear [Developer Name],

I hope this email finds you well. I wanted to take a moment to provide feedback on the code review for [Project Name]. Firstly, I wanted to commend you and the team on the excellent work that has been done so far. Your dedication and hard work are greatly appreciated.

During the code review, I noticed a few areas where we could make some improvements. Specifically, I think we can optimize the performance of some of the code by implementing a few changes. Additionally, there were a few sections where the code could be made more modular and easier to maintain.

I understand that these changes may require some additional effort on your part, but I strongly believe that they will greatly benefit the project in the long run. By improving the code quality and development efficiency, we can ensure that the project is completed on time and to the highest standards.

Please let me know if you have any questions or concerns regarding the feedback provided. I would be more than happy to discuss this with you further and provide any additional support that you may need.

Thank you again for your hard work and dedication to this project. I look forward to continuing to work with you to ensure its success.

Best regards,
[Your Name]

EMAIL 2: ALLOCATING RESOURCES FOR PROJECT SUCCESS

Allocating resources effectively is crucial to the success of any project, and it is the responsibility of the software project manager to ensure that the right resources are in place. In this specific situation, the software project manager is reaching out to functional managers to discuss resource allocation for a high-priority project. By analyzing project requirements and timelines, the manager has determined that additional resources are needed to ensure project success. The value of this email lies in its ability to prompt discussion and collaboration between the software project manager and functional managers, and to ensure that the project has the necessary resources to meet its goals. By doing so, the project manager can improve project timelines and success rates, and ultimately deliver a successful product to stakeholders.

Note: Effective communication is key in any project management role, and the ability to allocate resources effectively is essential to project success. This email highlights the importance of collaboration and communication between functional managers and software project managers, and the value of taking a proactive approach to resource allocation. By using a persuasive and friendly tone, the software project manager can encourage functional managers to engage in meaningful dialogue and work together to ensure project success.

Sample Email:

Subject Line: Resource Allocation for [Project Name]

Dear [Functional Manager Name],

I hope this email finds you well. I wanted to touch base with you regarding the resource allocation for [Project Name]. As you know, this project is a top priority for our organization, and it is crucial that we have the right resources allocated to it to ensure its success.

After a thorough analysis of the project requirements and timelines, I believe that we need to allocate additional resources to the project to ensure that we can meet our deadlines and deliver the highest quality product possible. Specifically, I think we need to bring in additional developers and QA specialists to help with the workload.

I understand that this may require some additional budget and resources, but I strongly believe that it is in the best interest of the project and our organization. By ensuring that we have the right resources allocated to the project, we can improve our project timelines and success rates, and ultimately deliver a successful product to our stakeholders.

Please let me know your thoughts on this matter, and if there are any concerns or questions that you may have. I look forward to discussing this further with you and finding the best possible solution to ensure the success of [Project Name].

Thank you for your time and attention to this matter.

Best regards,
[Your Name]

EMAIL 3: KEEPING THE BOSS INFORMED ON PROJECT PROGRESS

As a software project manager, it's crucial to keep your boss informed on the progress of your projects. Not only does this help to ensure that the project stays on track, but it also provides your boss with visibility into the work that you and your team are doing. By doing so, you can build trust and establish a better working relationship with your boss.

In this email, you have an opportunity to demonstrate your value as a project manager by providing a concise yet comprehensive update on the progress of the project. By highlighting the key achievements and potential challenges, you show that you are proactive in your approach to managing the project and have a clear understanding of the goals and objectives. Additionally, by offering to discuss any questions or concerns your boss may have, you demonstrate your willingness to collaborate and ensure alignment with the organization's goals.

Overall, by keeping your boss informed on project progress, you can improve communication, build trust, and ensure project success. This not only benefits the project but also demonstrates your value as a project manager and can help to advance your career.

Sample Email:

Subject Line: Project Status Update for [Project Name]

Dear [Boss Name],

I hope this email finds you well. I wanted to provide you with a quick update on the progress of [Project Name]. As you know, this project is a top priority for the company and I want to ensure that you are kept informed on its progress.

Overall, I am pleased to report that the project is progressing well. We have successfully completed the first phase of development and are now moving onto the second phase. The team is working hard to ensure that we stay on track and deliver the project on time.

I am also happy to report that we have encountered no major issues or setbacks thus far. However, we are closely monitoring the project and will keep you informed if any issues arise.

In terms of next steps, we will be focusing on completing the second phase of development and beginning the testing phase. I will keep you informed on our progress and ensure that we stay on track.

Please let me know if you have any questions or concerns regarding the project. I would be more than happy to discuss this with you further and provide any additional information that you may need.

Thank you for your continued support of this project. I look forward to updating you on our progress in the future.

Best regards,
[Your Name]

EMAIL 4: ENSURING TIMELY AND COST-EFFECTIVE CONTRACT RENEWALS WITH VENDORS

As a software project manager, one of your key responsibilities is to ensure that contracts with vendors are renewed in a timely and cost-effective manner. The benefits of successful contract renewals are numerous, including stronger relationships with vendors and improved procurement processes.

By negotiating favorable terms and exploring different options, such as bundling services or adjusting pricing structures, you can reduce costs while still maintaining the quality of the product or service. This not only benefits your company, but also strengthens your relationship with your vendor, leading to a more collaborative and successful partnership.

In addition, timely and cost-effective contract renewals can improve your procurement processes, ensuring that you have the necessary resources and services to support your software projects. This ultimately leads to improved project outcomes and stakeholder satisfaction.

Overall, prioritizing contract renewals and negotiating favorable terms is a critical component of successful software project management. By following the best practices outlined in the email template above, you can ensure that your contracts are renewed in a timely and cost-effective manner, leading to stronger vendor relationships and improved procurement processes.
Sample Email:

Subject Line: Contract Renewal Discussion for [Vendor Name]

Dear [Vendor Representative],

I hope this email finds you well. As we near the end of our current contract for [Product/Service Name], I wanted to discuss the possibility of renewing the contract for another term.

I have been pleased with the quality of your product/service and the level of support that your team has provided throughout the duration of our current contract. As such, I believe it would be in our mutual interest to continue our partnership.

In considering a contract renewal, I would like to explore the possibility of reducing costs where possible. Given the competitive nature of the market, it is important for us to ensure that we are getting the best value for our investment.

With this in mind, I would like to discuss the details of the contract and see if there are any areas where we can negotiate more favorable terms. I am open to exploring different options, such as bundling services, extending the contract term, or adjusting pricing structures.

I believe that a timely and cost-effective contract renewal will not only benefit our company, but also strengthen our relationship and improve our procurement processes. I look forward to discussing this further with you and exploring ways to continue our successful partnership.

Please let me know if you have any questions or concerns regarding the contract renewal. I would be more than happy to discuss this with you further and provide any additional information that you may need.

Thank you for your time and attention to this matter.

Best regards,
[Your Name]

EMAIL 5: SITUATION: PROVIDING PRODUCT DEMOS TO INCREASE SALES

As a software project manager, it's crucial to provide sales teams with the necessary tools and resources to sell products effectively. One such tool is a product demo, which can provide sales teams with a deeper understanding of the product's capabilities and unique value proposition. By showcasing the product's features and functionality, as well as its ability to solve specific customer challenges, sales teams can better communicate the value of the product to potential customers and close more deals. Through providing product demos, software project managers can help drive increased product sales and revenue, ultimately leading to the long-term success of the company.

Sample Email:

Subject Line: Product Demo for [Product Name]

Dear [Sales Team],

I hope this email finds you well. I am writing to provide you with a product demo for [Product Name]. As you know, this product is one of our key offerings, and it's crucial that we showcase its capabilities to potential customers.

During the demo, I will provide an overview of the product's features and functionality, as well as its unique value proposition. I will also walk you through some real-world use cases and demonstrate how the product can help solve specific customer challenges.

I believe that this demo will be incredibly valuable for you in your sales efforts. By gaining a deeper understanding of the product and its capabilities, you will be better equipped to communicate its value to potential customers and close more deals.

Please let me know if you have any questions or concerns regarding the demo. I would be more than happy to discuss this with you further and provide any additional support that you may need.

Thank you for your hard work and dedication to selling our products. I look forward to working with you to drive increased product sales and revenue.

Best regards,
[Your Name]

EMAIL 6: BUG FIX PRIORITIZATION FOR [PROJECT NAME]

Addressing critical bugs in a timely and efficient manner is crucial for improving product quality and customer satisfaction. As a software project manager, it is your responsibility to ensure that bugs are prioritized and addressed as soon as possible to ensure the success of the project.

Sample Email:

Subject Line: Bug Fix Prioritization for [Project Name]

Dear [Developer Name],

I hope this email finds you well. I wanted to discuss the prioritization of bug fixes for [Project Name]. As we move forward with the development of this project, it is important that we prioritize and address critical bugs in a timely and efficient manner.

I have reviewed the current bug list and identified a few critical bugs that are impacting the product quality and customer satisfaction. I would like to request that you and the team prioritize these bugs and work on them as soon as possible.

I understand that there may be other competing priorities and that fixing bugs can sometimes be challenging, but I strongly believe that addressing these critical bugs will greatly benefit the project in the long run. By improving the product quality and customer satisfaction, we can ensure that the project is successful and meets the needs of our users.

Please let me know if you have any questions or concerns regarding the bug prioritization. I would be more than happy to discuss this with you further and provide any additional support that you may need.

Thank you for your hard work and dedication to this project. I appreciate your efforts and look forward to working with you to ensure its success.

Best regards,
[Your Name]

EMAIL 7: ADDRESSING PROJECT REQUIREMENTS WITH FUNCTIONAL MANAGERS

As a software project manager, it is important to ensure that project requirements are being met in order to achieve project success and stakeholder satisfaction. In this email, you will learn how to effectively communicate with functional managers to identify areas of improvement and work together to address them. By doing so, you can improve project success rates and stakeholder satisfaction.

Sample Email:

Subject Line: Project Requirements Review for [Project Name]

Dear [Functional Manager Name],

I hope this email finds you well. As the software project manager for [Project Name], I wanted to touch base with you regarding the project requirements. As you know, meeting the requirements of our stakeholders is critical to the success of this project.

During our recent review, I noticed a few areas where we may not be fully meeting the requirements. Specifically, I think we need to focus on [list specific areas of concern or improvement here]. By addressing these areas, we can ensure that we are meeting the requirements of our stakeholders and delivering a successful project.

I wanted to take this opportunity to discuss these concerns with you and see how we can work together to address them. It is important that we are all on the same page when it comes to project requirements, and I believe that by working together, we can achieve this goal.

Please let me know if you have any questions or concerns regarding the project requirements. I would be more than happy to discuss this with you further and provide any additional support that you may need.

Thank you for your time and attention to this matter. I look forward to continuing to work with you to ensure the success of [Project Name].

Best regards,
[Your Name]

EMAIL 8: KEEPING YOUR BOSS INFORMED OF BUDGET UPDATES

Value: Managing project finances is crucial to the success of any project. Regular budget updates are necessary to ensure that the project stays on track and to prevent financial risks. It's important for a software project manager to provide regular budget updates to their boss to ensure transparency and effective financial planning. By keeping their boss informed, the project manager can ensure that they have the support they need to manage the budget effectively, identify cost-saving opportunities, and make informed decisions.

Sample Email:

Subject Line: Budget Update for [Project Name]

Dear [Boss's Name],

I hope this email finds you well. I wanted to take a moment to provide an update on the budget for [Project Name]. As we discussed in our last meeting, I have been closely monitoring project expenses and I am pleased to report that we are currently on track with our financial plan.

To date, we have spent [current expenditure amount] of the budgeted [total budget amount]. While there have been some unexpected expenses, we have been able to manage them within the overall budget. In addition, I have identified a few areas where we can make some cost-saving adjustments without impacting project quality or timelines.

I understand that budget management is a top priority for the success of this project and I will continue to keep a close eye on project finances. By ensuring financial planning and transparency, we can mitigate financial risks and make informed decisions.

Please let me know if you have any questions or concerns regarding the project budget. I would be more than happy to discuss this with you further and provide any additional support that you may need.

Thank you for your support and trust in my ability to manage the budget for [Project Name]. I look forward to our next meeting and discussing the progress of the project.

Best regards,
[Your Name]

EMAIL 9: REQUESTING NEW PRODUCT FEATURES FROM VENDORS

By reaching out to vendors to request new product features, software project managers can unlock the potential for improved product quality and customer satisfaction. By incorporating new and innovative features, software products can become more competitive in the market, increasing their value proposition and driving more sales. This can lead to increased revenue and improved customer retention, ultimately benefiting the company's bottom line.

However, requesting new product features from vendors can be a complex process, requiring careful planning and communication. As a software project manager, it's essential to approach vendors with a clear and compelling proposal that highlights the benefits of the new features and outlines the necessary steps to implement them successfully.

By utilizing the sample email provided and adapting it to your specific needs, you can ensure that your communication with vendors is clear, concise, and effective. This, in turn, can lead to successful partnerships and improved product quality, benefiting both the company and its customers.

Sample Email

Subject Line: New Product Feature Request for [Product Name]

Dear [Vendor Name],

I hope this email finds you well. I wanted to reach out to you today to discuss a potential new feature request for our [Product Name].

As you know, we are constantly looking for ways to improve our product and provide the best possible experience for our customers. After careful consideration, we have identified a need for a new feature that we believe would greatly enhance the value of our product.

Specifically, we are interested in incorporating [New Feature Request] into our product. We believe that this feature would greatly benefit our customers and improve their overall experience with our product.

I understand that incorporating new features can be a significant undertaking, and I wanted to discuss this request with you further. If this is something that you can accommodate, I would be happy to discuss the requirements and timeline in more detail.

Alternatively, if this is not something that you are able to accommodate, I would greatly appreciate your feedback and any suggestions you may have on alternative solutions.

Thank you for your time and consideration in this matter. I look forward to hearing back from you soon.

Best regards,
[Your Name]

EMAIL 10: NEW PRODUCT LAUNCH ANNOUNCEMENT TO SALES TEAM

Announcing a new product launch to the sales team is critical for generating excitement and interest in the product, ultimately leading to increased sales and revenue. By providing the sales team with the necessary information and support, they can effectively promote the product to customers and prospects. This email template provides a comprehensive announcement that highlights the key features and benefits of the new product, and encourages the sales team to share the product guide with customers and prospects. By doing so, they can generate interest and excitement, ultimately leading to increased sales and revenue for the company.

Sample Email:

Subject Line: New Product Launch Announcement for [Product Name]

Dear [Sales Team],

I am excited to announce the launch of our new product, [Product Name]. This has been an important project for our team, and we are thrilled to finally share it with our customers.

[Product Name] is a revolutionary new product that has been designed to meet the needs of our customers in a rapidly evolving market. It offers a range of innovative features that we believe will set it apart from the competition and provide our customers with the tools they need to succeed.

As part of the sales team, we rely on you to help us spread the word about this exciting new product. We are confident that [Product Name] will be a game-changer for our customers, and we need your help to ensure that it reaches as many people as possible.

To assist you in your efforts, we have created a comprehensive product guide that outlines the key features and benefits of [Product Name]. This guide is available for download on our website, and we encourage you to share it with your customers and prospects.

We are also happy to provide training and support to help you effectively promote [Product Name]. If you have any questions or need any assistance, please do not hesitate to reach out to us.

Thank you for your continued dedication to our company and for your support in this exciting new product launch. We look forward to working together to drive increased product sales and revenue.

Best regards,
[Your Name]

EMAIL 11: NEW TECHNOLOGY ADOPTION FOR IMPROVED PROJECT OUTCOMES

To successfully adopt new technologies, it is important to have a plan in place. By creating a detailed adoption plan, you can streamline the adoption process, identify potential risks, and create a training program to ensure everyone is up-to-speed. This not only helps you avoid potential pitfalls but also maximizes the benefits of the new technology. By leveraging an adoption plan, you can ensure that you are getting the most out of the new technology while minimizing any potential disruptions to your project.

Sample Email:

Subject Line: New Technology Adoption Plan for [Project Name]

Dear [Developer Name],

I hope this email finds you well. I wanted to discuss a new technology adoption plan for [Project Name]. As you know, the technology landscape is constantly evolving, and we need to stay up-to-date with the latest tools and frameworks to improve project efficiency and quality.

I have been researching some new technologies that I believe could greatly benefit our project, and I wanted to discuss them with you. Specifically, I think we should consider adopting [New Technology Name] to enhance our development capabilities and improve project outcomes.

I understand that adopting new technologies can be a challenge, but I strongly believe that it is worth the effort. By leveraging [New Technology Name], we can improve our development workflows, reduce time-to-market, and increase project efficiency and quality.

To successfully adopt this new technology, I would like to work with you and the team to create a plan for implementation. This plan will include assessing the skills needed to work with the new technology, identifying any potential risks, and creating a training program to ensure everyone is up-to-speed.

I welcome your thoughts and feedback on this proposal. If you have any questions or concerns, please let me know. I am confident that, by working together, we can successfully adopt this new technology and improve our project outcomes.

Thank you for your hard work and dedication to this project. I look forward to discussing this further with you.

Best regards,
[Your Name]

EMAIL 12: CHANGE MANAGEMENT PLAN FOR SOFTWARE PROJECTS

By having a strong change management plan in place, software project managers can improve project success rates and stakeholder satisfaction. With a plan in place, changes can be effectively managed, minimizing their impact on the project timeline, budget, and scope. Stakeholders can be kept informed of changes, and their expectations can be managed effectively. A well-executed change management plan can ensure that the project is completed on time and to the highest standards, providing value to both the company and its customers.

Sample Email

Subject Line: Change Management Plan for [Project Name]

Dear [Functional Manager Name],

I hope this email finds you well. As we move forward with [Project Name], I wanted to take a moment to discuss the importance of having a strong change management plan in place.

As you know, changes are an inevitable part of any project, and it is essential that we have a plan in place to effectively manage them. By proactively planning for changes that may affect the project, we can minimize their impact and ensure that the project stays on track.

To that end, I wanted to propose a change management plan that includes the following elements:

A clear process for requesting and reviewing changes
Criteria for evaluating the impact of proposed changes on the project timeline, budget, and scope
Procedures for communicating changes to stakeholders and managing their expectations
A process for implementing and testing changes to ensure they are properly integrated into the project
By having a strong change management plan in place, we can improve project success rates and stakeholder satisfaction. I believe that this plan will help us to effectively manage any changes that may arise and ensure that the project is completed on time and to the highest standards.

Please let me know if you have any questions or concerns regarding the proposed change management plan. I would be more than happy to discuss this with you further and provide any additional support that you may need.

Thank you for your time and attention to this matter. I look forward to continuing to work with you to ensure the success of [Project Name].

Best regards,
[Your Name]

EMAIL 13: MANAGE PROJECT RISKS FOR IMPROVED SUCCESS RATES

By proactively identifying and managing project risks, software project managers can greatly improve project success rates and stakeholder satisfaction. By addressing potential issues early on in the project and communicating them to stakeholders, project managers can minimize project delays, budget overruns, and quality issues. This can ultimately lead to increased customer satisfaction, improved vendor relationships, and increased revenue.

Sample Email:

Subject Line: Risk Assessment for [Project Name]

Dear [Boss Name],

I hope this email finds you well. I wanted to take a moment to discuss the risk assessment for [Project Name]. As the project manager, I believe it is essential to identify and manage project risks in order to ensure its success.

During the risk assessment, I identified several potential risks that could impact the project timeline and budget. These include the possibility of unforeseen technical issues, potential vendor delays, and changes in stakeholder requirements. I have also developed a plan to mitigate these risks, including additional testing and contingency planning.

I believe that by addressing these risks early on in the project, we can greatly improve its chances of success. By proactively managing potential issues and communicating them to stakeholders, we can ensure that the project is completed on time, within budget, and to the highest standards.

Please let me know if you have any questions or concerns regarding the risk assessment or mitigation plan. I would be more than happy to discuss this with you further and provide any additional information that you may need.

Thank you for your support and guidance throughout this project. I look forward to continuing to work with you to ensure its success.

Best regards,

[Your Name]

EMAIL 14: CONTRACT NEGOTIATION WITH VENDORS

By negotiating contracts with vendors, you can improve procurement processes and achieve cost savings for your company. This can lead to increased profitability and improved efficiency in project delivery. Furthermore, building strong relationships with vendors can lead to long-term partnerships that benefit both parties.

Sample Email:

Subject Line: Contract Negotiation for [Vendor Name]

Dear [Vendor Contact],

I hope this email finds you well. I wanted to discuss the contract negotiation for [Vendor Name] with you. As you know, our company values the partnership that we have with your organization and we would like to continue working together on future projects.

However, in order to ensure that our procurement processes are as efficient and cost-effective as possible, we need to negotiate terms that are favorable for both parties. Specifically, we are looking for more competitive pricing and improved delivery timelines for the products and services that your company provides.

We believe that our partnership is beneficial for both of our organizations and we would like to work with you to find a solution that meets both of our needs. Our goal is to establish a long-term relationship that is built on mutual respect and trust.

I would like to schedule a meeting with you to discuss the contract negotiation further. Please let me know what dates and times work best for you and we can arrange a time that is convenient for both of us.

Thank you for your attention to this matter. I look forward to hearing from you soon.

Best regards,
[Your Name]

EMAIL 15: PROVIDING COMPETITIVE ANALYSIS FOR IMPROVED SALES STRATEGY

A comprehensive competitive analysis is critical for a successful sales strategy. By identifying the strengths and weaknesses of our competitors, we can better position our product and highlight our unique value proposition. This allows us to differentiate ourselves in the market and increase sales and revenue. By leveraging this analysis, we can ensure that our sales team is equipped with the right information to make informed decisions and effectively communicate the value of our product to potential customers.

Sample Email:

Subject Line: Competitor Analysis for [Product Name]

Dear [Sales Team],

I hope this email finds you well. As part of our ongoing efforts to improve our sales strategy for [Product Name], I wanted to provide you with a competitive analysis that I believe will greatly benefit our sales efforts.

After conducting a thorough analysis of our competitors, I have identified a few key areas where we have a competitive advantage. Specifically, our product offers unique features and capabilities that are not currently available in the market. Additionally, we have a stronger brand presence and a proven track record of delivering high-quality products to our customers.

Based on this analysis, I recommend that we focus our sales efforts on highlighting these strengths and positioning ourselves as the clear choice for customers looking for a product that meets their needs and exceeds their expectations. By leveraging our competitive advantages, we can increase product sales and revenue and establish ourselves as a leader in the market.

I understand that competition in the market can be fierce, but I am confident that with the right approach and a focus on our strengths, we can achieve great success. As always, please let me know if you have any questions or concerns regarding this analysis or our sales strategy in general. I would be more than happy to discuss this with you further and provide any additional support that you may need.

Thank you for your hard work and dedication to selling [Product Name]. I look forward to continuing to work with you to drive its success.

Best regards,
[Your Name]

EMAIL 16: KEEPING YOUR DEVELOPMENT TEAM INFORMED

By keeping your development team informed of project timelines, you can improve communication and efficiency within your team. This enables team members to plan their work effectively, prioritize tasks, and stay on track to meet the project's goals and deadlines. Additionally, keeping the team informed fosters a sense of accountability and ownership over the project, which can lead to increased motivation and productivity.

Sample Email:

Subject Line: Development Timeline Update for [Project Name]

Dear [Developer Name],

I hope this email finds you well. I wanted to provide an update on the development timeline for [Project Name]. I understand that this information is critical for the development team to plan their work and ensure that the project is completed on time.

Based on the progress made so far, I am pleased to report that we are on track to meet our original timeline. However, I do want to emphasize the importance of keeping up the momentum and ensuring that we maintain the pace. As you know, any delay in the development process can have a significant impact on the project's overall success.

To that end, I want to remind the development team of the importance of maintaining effective communication and collaboration throughout the development process. If any issues or concerns arise that could impact the timeline, please bring them to my attention as soon as possible so that we can work together to find a solution.

I also want to encourage the team to continue working closely with the functional managers to ensure that all project requirements are met and the project's success criteria are achieved.

Thank you for your hard work and dedication to this project. I truly appreciate your contributions to its success, and I look forward to continuing to work with you to deliver a high-quality product.

Best regards,
[Your Name]

EMAIL 17: REQUESTING ADDITIONAL RESOURCES FOR PROJECT SUCCESS

As a software project manager, it's crucial to identify and request the necessary resources for your projects. By doing so, you can ensure that your project timelines are met and that the project is successful in achieving its goals. By sending a well-crafted email to functional managers, you can effectively communicate the need for additional resources and gain their support. This can lead to improved project success rates and ultimately benefit the company as a whole. A persuasive email that highlights the importance of additional resources and how they can impact the success of the project is key to gaining the support needed to move forward.

Sample Email:

Subject Line: Project Resource Requirements for [Project Name]

Dear [Functional Manager Name],

I hope this email finds you well. I wanted to discuss the resource requirements for [Project Name] with you. As the software project manager, it is my responsibility to identify and request the necessary resources for the project.

After careful analysis and review of the project plan, I have identified that we will require additional resources to ensure that we meet our timelines and achieve our goals. Specifically, we will need additional support from your department to provide the required expertise and manpower.

I understand that this may require some additional effort on your part, but I strongly believe that it will greatly benefit the project in the long run. By ensuring that we have the necessary resources, we can improve project timelines and success rates, which will benefit the company as a whole.

I would greatly appreciate it if you could review the project plan and provide me with your thoughts and feedback on the required resources. If there are any concerns or challenges that you foresee, please do not hesitate to let me know. I am more than happy to work with you to find a solution that meets the needs of both our teams.

Thank you for your time and consideration. I look forward to hearing back from you soon.

Best regards,
[Your Name]

EMAIL 18: PROVIDING FEEDBACK TO VENDORS ON PRODUCT DEMOS

Providing feedback to vendors on product demos is a critical component of successful vendor management. By providing constructive feedback, software project managers can ensure that vendor products are aligned with their needs and are of the highest quality. This feedback can also help to strengthen vendor relationships by demonstrating a commitment to collaboration and mutual success.

Sample Email:

Subject Line: Product Demo Feedback for [Product Name]

Dear [Vendor Name],

I hope this email finds you well. I wanted to take a moment to provide feedback on the product demo for [Product Name]. Firstly, I wanted to thank you and your team for taking the time to demo the product to us. Your dedication and hard work are greatly appreciated.

During the demo, I noticed a few areas where we could make some improvements. Specifically, I think there are a few features that could be added or improved upon to better meet our needs. Additionally, there were a few sections where the demo could be made more engaging and interactive.

I understand that these changes may require some additional effort on your part, but I strongly believe that they will greatly benefit both of our organizations in the long run. By improving the product quality and engagement of the demo, we can ensure that our partnership is successful and mutually beneficial.

Please let me know if you have any questions or concerns regarding the feedback provided. I would be more than happy to discuss this with you further and provide any additional support that you may need.

Thank you again for your hard work and dedication to our partnership. I look forward to continuing to work with you to ensure its success.

Best regards,
[Your Name]

EMAIL 19: PRICING STRATEGY UPDATE FOR [PRODUCT NAME]

In the highly competitive world of business, pricing strategies play a critical role in attracting and retaining customers. As a software project manager, it is important to keep your sales team updated on any changes to pricing strategies that can impact product sales and revenue. By providing timely updates, you can ensure that your sales team is equipped with the necessary information to effectively communicate the benefits of your products to customers. This can lead to increased product sales and revenue, and ultimately contribute to the success of your company. So, make sure to communicate any pricing strategy updates to your sales team and provide them with the support they need to effectively promote your products.

Sample Email:

Subject Line: Pricing Strategy Update for [Product Name]

Dear [Sales Team],

I hope this email finds you well. I wanted to take a moment to update you on our pricing strategy for [Product Name]. As you know, pricing is an important factor that can greatly impact product sales and revenue.

After careful consideration and analysis of market trends, we have decided to implement a new pricing strategy that we believe will better align with customer needs and expectations. This strategy involves a slight reduction in pricing for some of our products, which we anticipate will lead to an increase in sales and revenue.

I understand that this may require some adjustment on your part, and I want to assure you that we will provide all necessary support to ensure a smooth transition. We will be updating our marketing materials and sales collateral to reflect the new pricing strategy, and we will be providing training to help you effectively communicate the benefits of this strategy to our customers.

I am confident that this updated pricing strategy will have a positive impact on our sales and revenue. I encourage you to continue to promote [Product Name] to your customers and prospects, and to highlight the value that our products can provide.

Please let me know if you have any questions or concerns regarding the updated pricing strategy. I would be more than happy to discuss this with you further and provide any additional support that you may need.

Thank you for your hard work and dedication to promoting [Product Name]. I look forward to continuing to work with you to achieve our goals.

Best regards,

EMAIL 20: NEW FEATURE DEVELOPMENT PLAN FOR [PROJECT NAME]

By prioritizing and planning new features for the project, the software project manager can ensure improved product quality and customer satisfaction.

As a software project manager, planning and prioritizing new features for your project is a crucial aspect of ensuring its success. By doing so, you can ensure that your project meets the needs and expectations of your stakeholders and customers.

In this specific situation, you are tasked with creating a new feature development plan for [Project Name]. This plan will help you prioritize the most important features, assign them to the appropriate developers, and establish rough timelines for completion.

By creating a development plan, you can ensure that your team is working on the most important features first and that each feature is assigned to the best-suited developer. This will improve the quality of the product by ensuring that each feature is developed to the highest standards and meets the needs of your customers.

Furthermore, by completing the development of new features on time, you can improve customer satisfaction by delivering a product that meets or exceeds their expectations. This can lead to increased customer loyalty and improved sales.

Sample Email:

Subject Line: New Feature Development Plan for [Project Name]

Dear [Developer Name],

I hope this email finds you well. As we continue to work on [Project Name], I wanted to touch base with you regarding the development of new features. Our project stakeholders have expressed a strong interest in adding some new functionality to the product, and I believe that this will greatly benefit our customers.

As such, I wanted to outline a development plan for these new features. I have taken the time to prioritize the most important features, and have identified the development team members who will be responsible for each feature. I have also included some rough timelines for when each feature should be completed.

Here is a brief overview of the development plan:

Feature A - Assigned to [Developer Name] - Estimated Completion Date: [Date]
Feature B - Assigned to [Developer Name] - Estimated Completion Date: [Date]

Feature C - Assigned to [Developer Name] - Estimated Completion Date: [Date]
I understand that this development plan may be subject to change, but I believe that having a clear roadmap for these new features will greatly benefit our development efforts. By improving the product quality and customer satisfaction, we can ensure that [Project Name] is a success.

Please let me know if you have any questions or concerns regarding the development plan. I would be more than happy to discuss this with you further and provide any additional support that you may need.

Thank you for your hard work and dedication to this project. I look forward to continuing to work with you to ensure its success.

Best regards,
[Your Name]

EMAIL 21: PROJECT PERFORMANCE REVIEW FEEDBACK FOR IMPROVED SUCCESS RATES

As a software project manager, your goal is to ensure the success of your projects. One of the most effective ways to achieve this is through regular project performance reviews. By reviewing project progress and identifying areas for improvement, you can proactively address issues before they become major roadblocks. This not only improves project success rates but also enhances stakeholder satisfaction. By communicating feedback to functional managers and other team members, you can drive positive change and ensure that your project is delivered on time and to the highest standards. Don't wait until it's too late - make project performance reviews a regular part of your project management process and achieve success every time.

Sample Email

Subject Line: Project Performance Review for [Project Name]

Dear [Functional Manager Name],

I hope this email finds you well. As part of our ongoing efforts to ensure the success of [Project Name], I wanted to take a moment to review the project's performance to date.

Overall, the project has been progressing well, and we have achieved many of our key milestones on schedule. However, during the course of the review, I have identified a few areas where we can make some improvements.

Specifically, I believe that we could benefit from more frequent and transparent communication between the various teams involved in the project. By improving communication and collaboration, we can ensure that everyone is aligned with project goals and timelines, which will ultimately improve project success rates and stakeholder satisfaction.

Additionally, I think we could benefit from some additional training or resources to help us address some of the challenges that we have encountered during the project. For example, we could look into additional training for the team members involved in a specific area, or explore new tools or technologies that could help us work more efficiently.

I understand that these changes may require some additional effort on your part, but I strongly believe that they will greatly benefit the project in the long run. By identifying areas for improvement and proactively addressing them, we can ensure that we deliver the project on time and to the highest standards.

Please let me know if you have any questions or concerns regarding the feedback provided. I would be more than happy to discuss this with you further and provide any additional support that you may need.

Thank you for your continued support and dedication to the success of this project.

Best regards,

[Your Name]

EMAIL 22: TEAM PERFORMANCE REVIEW

A team performance review can provide significant value to your project by identifying areas for improvement, such as communication, training, or resource allocation. By addressing these areas, you can improve your team's efficiency and productivity, ultimately leading to improved project success rates and stakeholder satisfaction. Additionally, a team performance review can help recognize and celebrate team strengths, which can boost team morale and foster a positive work culture.

Conducting a team performance review may seem daunting, but it doesn't have to be. By using a standardized approach and providing constructive feedback, you can ensure that your team is on track to meet project goals and achieve success. As a software project manager, investing the time and effort into a team performance review is well worth it for the improved project outcomes it can generate.

Sample Email:

Subject Line: Team Performance Review for [Team Name]

Dear [Boss's Name],

I hope this email finds you well. I wanted to take a moment to provide you with a team performance review for [Team Name]. As the software project manager, I have been closely monitoring the team's performance and have identified a few areas where we can make some improvements.

Overall, I have been impressed with the team's efficiency and productivity. The team has been working hard to deliver on our project goals and has been consistently meeting deadlines. However, I have noticed a few areas where we can improve.

Firstly, I think that we can benefit from more regular team meetings to discuss project progress, identify potential roadblocks, and ensure that everyone is aligned with our project goals. Additionally, I think that we can benefit from additional training or professional development opportunities to enhance our skills and knowledge.

I strongly believe that by addressing these areas of improvement, we can further improve the team's efficiency and productivity. I am committed to working closely with the team to implement these changes and ensure that we are continuously improving.

Please let me know if you have any questions or concerns regarding the team performance review. I would be more than happy to discuss this with you further and provide any additional information that you may need.

Thank you for your ongoing support of our team and project. I look forward to continuing to work together to ensure its success.

Best regards,
[Your Name]

EMAIL 23: IMPROVING PRODUCT QUALITY AND CUSTOMER SATISFACTION THROUGH VENDOR SUGGESTIONS

Collaborating with vendors to improve product quality and customer satisfaction can provide several benefits for software project managers. Firstly, it can help you stay ahead of the competition by delivering products that meet the evolving needs and preferences of your customers. This can ultimately lead to increased sales and revenue.

Secondly, it can help you build strong and lasting relationships with your vendors. By working together towards a common goal, you can foster a sense of trust and partnership that can lead to more successful collaborations in the future.

Finally, it can help you improve the overall quality of your products and ensure customer satisfaction. By listening to feedback and suggestions from vendors, you can identify potential areas for improvement and implement changes that will benefit your customers.

Sample Email:

Subject Line: Product Improvement Suggestions for [Product Name]

Dear [Vendor Name],

I hope this email finds you well. I wanted to take a moment to provide some suggestions for improving [Product Name]. We value our partnership with you and we believe that these suggestions can greatly benefit the product quality and overall customer satisfaction.

Firstly, I suggest that we work together to improve the user interface of the product. This can be achieved by enhancing the visual design and layout to create a more intuitive and user-friendly experience for our customers. Additionally, we believe that adding more robust functionality to the product would greatly enhance its value and usefulness for our customers.

Furthermore, we suggest that we work together to improve the product's performance and reliability. By identifying and addressing any potential issues or bottlenecks, we can ensure that the product runs smoothly and meets the needs of our customers.

We understand that these improvements may require some additional effort on your part, but we believe that they are crucial to ensuring the success of the product and our partnership. We look forward to discussing these suggestions with you further and working together to make them a reality.

Thank you for your attention to this matter. We value our partnership with you and we believe that by working together, we can achieve great success with [Product Name].

Best regards,
[Your Name]

EMAIL 24: SALES FORECAST UPDATE FOR [PRODUCT NAME]

By providing regular updates on sales forecasts to the sales team, software project managers can ensure that everyone is on the same page and working towards the same goals. This can help to improve sales planning and revenue projections, which can ultimately lead to increased profitability for the company.

Regular sales forecast updates can also help the sales team to better understand the market trends and customer needs, which can inform their sales strategies and lead to more effective promotions. By keeping the team informed and engaged, software project managers can create a sense of shared ownership over the success of the product, which can improve motivation and productivity.

In addition, sales forecast updates can help to identify areas where additional resources or support may be required. For example, if sales forecasts are lower than expected, this may signal the need for additional marketing efforts or changes to the product itself. By staying up-to-date on sales forecasts, software project managers can proactively address any issues and keep the project on track towards success.

Sample Email:

Subject Line: Sales Forecast Update for [Product Name]

Dear [Sales Team],

I hope this email finds you well. I wanted to provide you with an update on the sales forecast for [Product Name]. As you know, this product is a key focus for the company, and I wanted to ensure that everyone is up-to-date on our revenue projections.

After reviewing the latest market trends and analyzing customer feedback, I am pleased to report that we are seeing strong demand for [Product Name]. Our sales forecasts have been revised accordingly, and we now anticipate sales to exceed our initial projections.

To capitalize on this opportunity, I would like to request that the sales team increase their efforts in promoting [Product Name]. This could include reaching out to potential clients, offering special promotions, or providing more targeted marketing campaigns. I am confident that these efforts will lead to even greater success for the product.

As always, please let me know if you have any questions or concerns. I am available to discuss this further and provide any additional support that may be required.

Thank you for your hard work and dedication to the success of [Product Name]. I look forward to continuing to work together to achieve our sales goals.

RAHUL PARMAR

Best regards,
[Your Name]

EMAIL 25: CODING STANDARDS REVIEW REQUEST

Ensuring code quality and development efficiency is critical to the success of any software project. Adhering to coding standards is a key factor in achieving these goals. By performing a coding standards review for your project, you can identify any areas where the code may not be in compliance with your standards and make necessary changes. This not only ensures high-quality code but also makes it easier for developers to understand and maintain the code. Ultimately, this leads to improved development efficiency and a more successful project outcome.

Sample Email:

Subject Line: Coding Standards Review for [Project Name]

Dear [Developer Name],

I hope this email finds you well. As we continue to work on [Project Name], I wanted to take a moment to discuss the importance of adhering to coding standards.

Following coding standards is critical to ensuring high-quality code and development efficiency. Consistent code formatting and style make it easier for developers to understand and maintain the code. Additionally, adhering to standards can prevent issues such as bugs, errors, and security vulnerabilities.

As such, I would like to request that we perform a coding standards review for [Project Name]. This review will help us identify any areas where the code may not be in compliance with our standards, and allow us to make any necessary changes.

I understand that this review may require some additional effort on your part, but I strongly believe that it will greatly benefit the project in the long run. By adhering to coding standards, we can ensure that the project is completed on time and to the highest standards.

Please let me know if you have any questions or concerns regarding the coding standards review. I would be more than happy to discuss this with you further and provide any additional support that you may need.

Thank you for your hard work and dedication to this project. I look forward to continuing to work with you to ensure its success.

Best regards,
[Your Name]

EMAIL 26: PROJECT SCHEDULE REVIEW FOR [PROJECT NAME]

Effective project management requires a keen eye for detail and the ability to identify potential issues before they become major problems. A project schedule review is a critical tool that software project managers can use to achieve this goal.

By reviewing project schedules, you can identify potential delays and take proactive steps to mitigate them. This ensures that your projects stay on track and are completed on time and within budget. Additionally, regular schedule reviews can help you identify trends and patterns that may impact future projects, allowing you to make informed decisions about resource allocation and project planning.

Sample Email:

Subject Line: Project Schedule Review for [Project Name]

Dear [Functional Manager Name],

I hope this email finds you well. I wanted to take a moment to review the project schedule for [Project Name] and provide some feedback. As you know, the success of the project depends greatly on our ability to meet the established timelines.

During my review, I noticed that there may be some potential delays in the project schedule. Specifically, there are a few tasks that may require additional resources or have dependencies that could cause delays. Additionally, I noticed that some of the timelines may be a bit optimistic given the complexity of the project.

I understand that delays and changes to the schedule can be frustrating for everyone involved. However, it is important that we identify these potential issues early on so that we can take appropriate actions to mitigate them. By addressing these issues proactively, we can ensure that the project is completed on time and to the highest standards.

I would appreciate it if you could review the schedule and provide any additional feedback or insights that you may have. Together, we can work to identify any potential issues and make the necessary adjustments to keep the project on track.

Thank you for your attention to this matter. I look forward to continuing to work with you to ensure the success of [Project Name].

Best regards,
[Your Name]

EMAIL 27: NEED TO COMMUNICATE PROJECT DELIVERY PLANS TO BOSS

Effective project delivery planning is crucial for project success. A well-defined project delivery plan provides a clear roadmap for the project and ensures that all stakeholders are aligned and informed about the project status. This leads to improved project outcomes, increased stakeholder satisfaction, and improved project success rates. By creating and communicating project delivery plans to your boss, you can ensure that everyone is on the same page and working towards the same goals. This helps to minimize project risks and optimize project outcomes, leading to a successful project delivery.

Sample Email:

Subject Line: Project Delivery Plan for [Project Name]

Dear [Boss's Name],

I am writing to provide you with an update on the project delivery plan for [Project Name]. As the software project manager, it is my responsibility to ensure that the project is delivered on time and to the highest standards. In order to achieve this, I have created a detailed project delivery plan that outlines the key milestones, deadlines, and deliverables for the project.

The project delivery plan includes a comprehensive list of tasks, along with their timelines and dependencies. This will help us to manage the project more efficiently and effectively, and ensure that we meet all project goals and objectives.

Additionally, the plan includes a risk management strategy that identifies potential risks and outlines mitigation plans to address them. By proactively managing risks, we can minimize the impact of any unforeseen issues and ensure that the project stays on track.

I believe that this project delivery plan will greatly benefit the project and improve its success rates. By providing a clear roadmap for the project, we can ensure that all stakeholders are aligned and informed about the project status. This will increase stakeholder satisfaction and improve overall project outcomes.

Please let me know if you have any questions or concerns regarding the project delivery plan. I would be more than happy to discuss this with you further and provide any additional information that you may need.

Thank you for your continued support and guidance. I look forward to delivering a successful project.

Best regards,

[Your Name]

EMAIL 28: VENDOR PERFORMANCE REVIEW

When you review vendor performance, you not only provide valuable feedback that can help them improve their services, but you also demonstrate your commitment to ensuring the success of your projects. By addressing issues and working collaboratively with your vendors, you can build stronger relationships that are based on trust and mutual respect.

In addition, by improving your procurement processes, you can ensure that you are getting the best possible value for your organization. By identifying areas where vendors can improve, you can negotiate better contracts and ensure that you are working with the most qualified and reliable partners.

Sample Email:

Subject Line: Vendor Performance Review for [Vendor Name]

Dear [Vendor Name],

I hope this email finds you well. I wanted to take a moment to discuss our recent partnership and provide some feedback on your performance as a vendor for our company.

Overall, I have been pleased with the quality of your work and your responsiveness to our needs. Your team has demonstrated a high level of expertise and professionalism, which has been greatly appreciated.

However, I would like to bring to your attention a few areas where we believe improvements can be made. Specifically, we have identified some instances where communication could have been clearer and more timely. Additionally, there have been a few instances where deadlines were missed, which caused some delays in our project timeline.

I understand that these issues may be the result of a variety of factors, but it is important that we work together to address them. By improving your performance in these areas, we can ensure that our procurement processes are more efficient and that our partnership remains strong.

I would be happy to discuss these issues with you in more detail and provide any additional feedback that you may need. I value our partnership and want to ensure that we are working together to achieve the best possible outcomes for both of our organizations.

Thank you for your time and attention to this matter.

Best regards,
[Your Name]

EMAIL 29: PRODUCT ROADMAP UPDATE FOR [PRODUCT NAME]

Keeping your sales team informed of product roadmap updates is critical to the success of your product. By providing regular updates, you can ensure that the sales team is prepared to answer customer questions, address concerns, and promote the product effectively. This not only leads to increased sales but also improves customer satisfaction and loyalty. In this email, you will learn how to effectively communicate product roadmap updates to your sales team, providing them with the information they need to promote your product successfully.

Sample Email:

Subject Line: Product Roadmap Update for [Product Name]

Dear [Sales Team],

I hope this email finds you well. I wanted to take a moment to provide an update on the product roadmap for [Product Name]. As we continue to work on this project, it is important that we keep the sales team informed of any updates and changes to the product roadmap.

I am happy to report that we are making great progress on the project and we have a clear roadmap for the upcoming months. We have identified several key features that we believe will greatly enhance the product and improve its sales potential. These features include [feature 1], [feature 2], and [feature 3].

In addition to these new features, we have also made some updates to the existing features based on customer feedback and market trends. We believe that these updates will make the product even more competitive and appealing to potential customers.

Overall, we are very excited about the direction that the project is headed and we believe that these updates will greatly improve the product's sales potential. As always, we are open to feedback and suggestions from the sales team and we welcome your thoughts on these updates.

Please let me know if you have any questions or concerns regarding the product roadmap update. I would be more than happy to discuss this with you further and provide any additional support that you may need.

Thank you for your hard work and dedication to the success of [Product Name]. I look forward to continuing to work with you to achieve our sales goals.

Best regards,
[Your Name]

EMAIL 30: TESTING PLAN REVIEW FOR [PROJECT NAME]

By conducting a thorough review of the testing plan, you can identify potential gaps or deficiencies in the testing process and make the necessary adjustments to ensure that all areas of the product are thoroughly tested. This can result in improved product quality, fewer issues reported by customers, and increased customer satisfaction. By addressing these issues proactively, you can avoid potential delays in the release of the product, reduce the cost of fixing issues, and ensure the long-term success of your project. So, take the time to review your testing plan and make any necessary adjustments to ensure a successful release.

Sample Email:

Subject Line: Testing Plan Review for [Project Name]

Dear [Developer Name],

I hope this email finds you well. As we approach the final stages of [Project Name], I wanted to take a moment to review the testing plan and ensure that we are on track for a successful release.

I understand that the testing phase can be tedious, but it is a critical component in ensuring the high quality of our product. That's why it's important that we follow the testing plan closely to ensure that all aspects of the product have been thoroughly tested and meet the required standards.

During my review of the testing plan, I noticed that there were a few areas where the testing could be more comprehensive. Specifically, I think we should focus on the areas that are most critical to the customer experience and ensure that we have robust test cases for each scenario.

I appreciate your hard work in following the testing plan so far, and I encourage you to continue doing so. If you have any questions or concerns regarding the testing plan or testing process, please don't hesitate to reach out to me or the testing team.

By adhering to the testing plan and ensuring that all areas of the product are thoroughly tested, we can improve product quality and customer satisfaction. Thank you for your dedication to this project, and I look forward to working with you to ensure its success.

Best regards,
[Your Name]

EMAIL 31: IMPORTANCE OF RISK MITIGATION PLANNING IN SOFTWARE PROJECTS

Effective risk mitigation planning is crucial to the success of any software project. By proactively identifying potential risks and developing strategies to mitigate them, software project managers can improve project success rates and increase stakeholder satisfaction. Risk mitigation planning allows software project managers to minimize project disruptions and delays, prevent financial losses, and ensure the timely delivery of high-quality projects. Additionally, it enables software project managers to make informed decisions about project timelines, budgets, and resource allocation. By prioritizing risk mitigation planning, software project managers can avoid potential pitfalls and position their projects for long-term success.

Sample Email:

Subject Line: Risk Mitigation Plan for [Project Name]

Dear [Functional Manager Name],

I hope this email finds you well. I wanted to discuss the importance of creating a risk mitigation plan for [Project Name]. As you know, effective risk management is crucial to the success of any project. By identifying potential risks and developing a plan to mitigate them, we can improve the project's success rates and increase stakeholder satisfaction.

In order to create an effective risk mitigation plan, we need to identify potential risks and assess their likelihood and impact. Once we have identified these risks, we can develop strategies to minimize or eliminate them. This may involve developing contingency plans, adjusting project timelines, or allocating additional resources as needed.

I believe that it is important for us to work together to create a comprehensive risk mitigation plan for [Project Name]. This will help us to proactively manage potential risks and ensure that the project is completed on time and to the highest standards.

Please let me know your thoughts on this matter, and if you have any suggestions or concerns regarding the development of a risk mitigation plan. I look forward to working with you to ensure the success of [Project Name].

Best regards,
[Your Name]

EMAIL 32: FORECASTING PROJECT BUDGETS

Forecasting project budgets provides many benefits for both project managers and stakeholders. By accurately predicting costs, project managers can allocate resources effectively, make informed decisions about project scope, and ensure that the project stays within budget. This provides stakeholders with transparency, and confidence in the project's financial viability. Forecasting project budgets can also help identify potential areas for cost savings, allowing project managers to adjust the project plan accordingly. In short, forecasting project budgets is a critical tool for project managers looking to improve financial planning, transparency, and the overall success of their projects.

Sample Email:

Subject Line: Project Budget Forecast for [Project Name]

Dear [Boss's Name],

I hope this email finds you well. As we move forward with the [Project Name] project, I wanted to provide you with a project budget forecast to ensure that we stay on track financially and avoid any surprises down the line.

Based on the current project plan and the estimated costs for each stage, I have forecasted the total project budget to be [$Budget Amount]. This includes all anticipated costs, such as salaries, hardware and software purchases, and other project-related expenses.

I have attached a detailed breakdown of the forecasted costs, along with an explanation of the assumptions and risks associated with the forecast. Please review this information and let me know if you have any questions or concerns. Additionally, if there are any changes in the project scope or timeline, I will be sure to update the forecast accordingly and communicate any potential impact to the budget.

By forecasting the project budget, we can ensure improved financial planning and transparency, and avoid any surprises or unexpected costs. I believe this will be a valuable tool for us as we move forward with the project.

Thank you for your time and consideration. Please let me know if you require any additional information or support.

Best regards,
[Your Name]

EMAIL 33: CONTRACT TERMINATION WITH VENDORS

The value of handling a contract termination with vendors smoothly cannot be overstated. By doing so, you can maintain positive vendor relationships and ensure that the termination does not negatively impact the project. This can lead to improved vendor procurement processes and the ability to work with the vendor again in the future.

One way to handle a contract termination smoothly is to use the right words in your communication with the vendor. Our sample email provides an example of how to do this effectively, emphasizing that the decision is not a reflection of the vendor's quality of work and expressing a desire to work together in the future. By following these guidelines and using the right communication strategies, you can navigate contract termination discussions with vendors in a way that benefits both parties.

Sample Email:

Subject Line: Contract Termination Discussion for [Vendor Name]

Dear [Vendor Name],

I hope this email finds you well. I wanted to touch base with you regarding our current contract and discuss the possibility of terminating it.

While it was a difficult decision, we have determined that it is in the best interest of the project to end our contract with your company. This decision was based on a variety of factors, including changes in project scope and budget, as well as a shift in our vendor procurement processes.

I want to emphasize that this decision is not a reflection on the quality of work that your company has provided thus far. In fact, we have been very pleased with the level of service that you have provided, and we hope that this can be the start of a continued positive relationship between our companies.

Moving forward, we would like to discuss the best way to proceed with the contract termination. Specifically, we would like to work with you to ensure a smooth transition of any outstanding work, as well as discuss any outstanding invoices or payments.

Please let us know your availability to discuss these matters further. We appreciate your cooperation and understanding during this process.

Thank you for your time and efforts on this project. We wish you and your company all the best in your future endeavors.

Best regards,
[Your Name]

EMAIL 34: MARKETING PLAN REVIEW FOR [PRODUCT NAME]

As a software project manager, it is important to review the marketing plans for your products to ensure maximum visibility and drive more sales. By reviewing the marketing plan, you can identify areas for improvement, such as messaging and marketing channels, that can help you reach your target audience more effectively. Making these improvements can increase the visibility of the product and drive more sales, ultimately leading to increased revenue for the company. With effective communication and collaboration with the sales team, you can make the necessary improvements and ensure a successful launch for your product.

Sample Email:

Subject Line: Review of Marketing Plan for [Product Name]

Dear [Sales Team Name],

I hope this email finds you well. As we continue to work towards the launch of [Product Name], I wanted to take a moment to review the current marketing plan and identify areas for improvement.

Firstly, I would like to commend you on the great work that has been done so far. The marketing plan is well thought out, and it is evident that a lot of time and effort has gone into it. However, there are a few areas where we can make some improvements to ensure that we maximize the potential of this product.

One area where we can improve is in the messaging. While the messaging is good, I believe we can make it more compelling and customer-focused. We want to ensure that we are communicating the unique benefits of the product effectively and resonating with the target audience.

Another area where we can improve is in the marketing channels that we are utilizing. While we are currently using a variety of channels, I think we can explore additional channels that may be more effective in reaching our target audience.

By making these improvements, we can increase the visibility of the product and drive more sales, which will ultimately lead to increased revenue for the company.

I would love to hear your thoughts on these areas for improvement and any other ideas that you may have. Let's work together to ensure that we have a successful launch for [Product Name].

Thank you for your hard work and dedication to this project.

Best regards,
[Your Name]

EMAIL 35: TECHNICAL DEBT MANAGEMENT PLAN

By proactively managing technical debt, software project managers can improve product quality and development efficiency. A technical debt management plan outlines a strategy for identifying and addressing technical debt in a timely and efficient manner, ultimately ensuring that the project is completed on time and to the highest standards. Prioritizing necessary tasks and addressing technical debt as it arises can help avoid costly delays and errors, and ultimately lead to higher quality products and greater customer satisfaction. With an effective technical debt management plan in place, software project managers can stay ahead of potential issues and deliver successful projects every time.

Sample Email:

Subject Line: Technical Debt Management Plan for [Project Name]

Dear [Developer Name],

I hope this email finds you well. As we move forward with [Project Name], I wanted to discuss the importance of managing technical debt and prioritizing necessary tasks. Technical debt can accumulate quickly and negatively impact product quality and development efficiency, which is why it's important to have a plan in place to manage it effectively.

To that end, I would like to propose a technical debt management plan for [Project Name]. This plan will outline a strategy for identifying and addressing technical debt in a timely and efficient manner. By prioritizing necessary tasks and addressing technical debt as it arises, we can ensure that the project is completed on time and to the highest standards.

I understand that managing technical debt can be a challenging task, but I believe that it's essential to the success of this project. By taking the time to proactively manage technical debt, we can improve product quality and development efficiency, which will ultimately benefit the entire team.

Please let me know if you have any questions or concerns regarding this plan. I would be happy to discuss this with you further and provide any additional support that you may need.

Thank you for your hard work and dedication to this project. I look forward to continuing to work with you to ensure its success.

Best regards,
[Your Name]

EMAIL 36: PROJECT QUALITY ASSURANCE REVIEW FOR [PROJECT NAME]

By conducting a project quality assurance review, you can proactively identify and address any potential quality issues before they impact the project's success. This not only results in improved product quality but also increases customer satisfaction. By addressing quality issues early on, you can ensure that the project is delivered on time, within budget, and to the highest quality standards. This, in turn, leads to happy customers and a successful project outcome. So, if you want to ensure that your projects are of the highest quality, conducting regular project quality assurance reviews is a must!

Sample Email:

Subject Line: Project Quality Assurance Review for [Project Name]

Dear [Functional Manager Name],

I hope this email finds you well. I wanted to reach out to you to discuss the project quality assurance for [Project Name]. As the software project manager, it's important to ensure that we are maintaining the highest quality standards throughout the project lifecycle.

To that end, I would like to schedule a meeting with you to review the project quality assurance measures that are currently in place. This will allow us to identify any gaps or areas where we can improve to ensure that the project meets our quality objectives.

By conducting this review, we can proactively identify and address any potential quality issues before they impact the project's success. Ultimately, this will result in an improved product quality and increased customer satisfaction.

I would greatly appreciate it if you could let me know your availability for a meeting in the next few days. Please let me know if there are any specific items that you would like to discuss during the meeting.

Thank you for your attention to this matter, and I look forward to hearing from you soon.

Best regards,
[Your Name]

EMAIL 37: PROJECT GOVERNANCE PLAN

A project governance plan is essential to ensure the success of any project. It outlines the processes and procedures that will be followed throughout the project lifecycle to ensure that objectives are met and the project is delivered on time and within budget. It also ensures that everyone is on the same page and that there is clear communication and understanding of expectations. By having a project governance plan in place, risks and issues can be managed effectively, changes can be responded to in a timely manner, and project success rates and stakeholder satisfaction can be improved. A well-executed project governance plan will help project managers and stakeholders stay aligned and focused on achieving project objectives.

Sample Email:

Subject Line: Project Governance Plan for [Project Name]

Dear [Boss's Name],

I wanted to take a moment to discuss the project governance plan for [Project Name] that I have developed. As you are aware, effective project governance is essential to ensure the success of any project, and I believe that the plan I have put together will help us achieve this goal.

The project governance plan outlines the processes and procedures that we will follow throughout the project lifecycle to ensure that we meet our objectives and deliver the project on time and within budget. It includes details on the roles and responsibilities of key stakeholders, the decision-making processes that will be used, and the metrics that we will use to measure project success.

One of the key benefits of having a project governance plan in place is that it ensures that everyone is on the same page and that there is clear communication and understanding of expectations. This leads to improved project success rates and stakeholder satisfaction, as we are able to manage risks and issues effectively and respond to changes in a timely manner.

I believe that the project governance plan I have developed is comprehensive and effective, and I would be happy to walk you through the details and answer any questions you may have. I am confident that with this plan in place, we will be able to deliver a successful project that meets the needs of our stakeholders.

Thank you for your time and consideration. I look forward to discussing this further with you.

Best regards,
[Your Name]

EMAIL 38: REQUESTING PRODUCT FEATURES FROM VENDORS

Requesting product features from vendors is essential for improving product quality and customer satisfaction. By communicating your specific needs and preferences to your vendors, you can ensure that your product meets the requirements of your customers and remains competitive in the market. Effective communication with vendors is also critical for building and maintaining strong business relationships. By working together to identify and implement new product features, you can demonstrate your commitment to innovation and customer satisfaction, which can lead to increased sales and revenue.

Sample Email:

Subject Line: Product Feature Request for [Product Name]

Dear [Vendor Name],

I hope this email finds you well. I wanted to take a moment to discuss a few product features that we believe would greatly benefit [Product Name]. As you know, our goal is to provide our customers with the highest quality products and services, and we believe that these features would help us achieve that goal.

Firstly, we would like to request a new feature that would allow for easier integration with third-party software. We have received feedback from several customers that this would greatly improve their experience with the product.

Secondly, we would like to request a feature that would allow for greater customization options. This would enable our customers to tailor the product to their specific needs and preferences, thereby increasing their satisfaction with the product.

Finally, we would like to request a feature that would improve the overall performance of the product. We believe that by making some adjustments to the code, we can achieve significant improvements in speed and efficiency, which would benefit both us and our customers.

We understand that these requests may require some additional effort on your part, but we believe that they are essential for improving the product quality and customer satisfaction. We value our partnership with your company and appreciate your continued support in providing the best products and services to our customers.

Please let us know if you have any questions or concerns regarding these requests. We look forward to hearing from you and working together to make [Product Name] even better.

Thank you for your time and consideration.

Best regards,

RAHUL PARMAR

[Your Name]

EMAIL 39: DEVELOPING A PRODUCT DIFFERENTIATION STRATEGY FOR [PRODUCT NAME]

Developing a product differentiation strategy is crucial in today's highly competitive market to increase sales and revenue. By identifying the unique features and benefits of your product and communicating them effectively to your customers, you can set yourself apart from the competition and better meet the needs of your target audience. This not only increases brand awareness and demand but also establishes your product as the go-to solution for customers' needs, resulting in increased sales and revenue. A well-executed product differentiation strategy can help you achieve long-term success and maintain your competitive edge in the market.

Sample Email:

Subject Line: Product Differentiation Strategy for [Product Name]

Dear [Sales Team],

I hope this email finds you well. I wanted to take a moment to discuss a crucial aspect of our product strategy: differentiation. With the ever-increasing competition in the market, it is crucial that we differentiate our product from the competition.

I believe that developing a product differentiation strategy for [Product Name] will be crucial in increasing our product sales and revenue. By highlighting the unique features and benefits of our product, we can set ourselves apart from the competition and better meet the needs of our customers.

To start developing this strategy, I suggest that we conduct a market analysis to better understand our customers and their needs. We can also leverage customer feedback and data to identify areas where we can differentiate our product from the competition.

Once we have identified our unique selling proposition, we can work together to develop effective messaging and marketing materials to communicate this to our customers. This will help us to increase brand awareness, drive demand, and ultimately increase sales and revenue.

I am committed to working closely with you to develop and implement a successful product differentiation strategy for [Product Name]. Please let me know if you have any questions or concerns regarding this strategy, and I would be happy to discuss this further with you.

Thank you for your dedication and hard work in selling our products, and I look forward to working with you to achieve even greater success.

Best regards,
[Your Name]

EMAIL 40: NEED FOR A COMPREHENSIVE RELEASE MANAGEMENT PLAN

In today's fast-paced world, efficient and effective release management is critical to the success of any software project. A well-planned and executed release process can significantly improve the quality of the product, increase customer satisfaction, and ultimately drive revenue growth. By having a comprehensive release management plan in place, software project managers can ensure that their products are delivered on time, within budget, and to the highest standards. With a well-organized and efficient release process, project managers can save time, reduce costs, and improve stakeholder satisfaction. So, if you're a software project manager looking to improve your release management process and deliver successful projects, it's time to invest in a comprehensive release management plan.

Sample Email:

Subject Line: Release Management Plan for [Project Name]

Dear [Developer Name],

I hope this email finds you well. I wanted to discuss the release management plan for [Project Name] with you. As we approach the release date, it is crucial that we have a comprehensive plan in place to ensure a successful launch.

To that end, I have created a release management plan that outlines the necessary steps and timelines for the release process. This plan includes a detailed schedule of release milestones, quality assurance testing, and stakeholder communication.

I believe that this plan will greatly improve the quality of our product and increase customer satisfaction. By having a well-organized and efficient release process, we can ensure that our product is delivered on time, within budget, and to the highest standards.

I would like to review the plan with you in more detail during our next meeting to ensure that we are aligned and that all necessary steps have been accounted for. Additionally, please let me know if you have any feedback or suggestions to improve the plan further.

Thank you for your hard work and dedication to this project. I am confident that with a well-executed release management plan, we will achieve our goals and deliver a high-quality product to our customers.

Best regards,
[Your Name]

EMAIL 41: CONDUCTING A COST-BENEFIT ANALYSIS FOR A PROJECT

Conducting a cost-benefit analysis for a project is an essential step in ensuring the project's success and maximum return on investment. A cost-benefit analysis provides an in-depth understanding of the financial implications of the project and helps stakeholders make informed decisions about resource allocation and project timelines. By conducting this analysis, project managers can identify potential risks and challenges, monitor them closely, and take appropriate measures to mitigate them. Additionally, a cost-benefit analysis provides transparency and helps organizations plan their finances better. Ultimately, the value of conducting a cost-benefit analysis lies in improved financial planning, increased transparency, and ensuring that the project is completed on time, within budget, and to the highest standards.

Sample Email:

Subject Line: Project Cost-Benefit Analysis for [Project Name]

Dear [Functional Manager Name],

I hope this email finds you well. I wanted to touch base with you regarding the cost-benefit analysis for [Project Name]. As you know, conducting a cost-benefit analysis is an essential part of project planning and can help us make informed decisions about resource allocation and project timelines.

I wanted to provide you with a brief overview of the analysis and the key findings. Our analysis indicates that the project will have a significant positive impact on our organization's financial performance, and the benefits far outweigh the costs. In particular, we identified several areas where the project will help us improve our operational efficiency and reduce costs.

However, I also wanted to bring to your attention a few areas where we identified potential risks and challenges. Specifically, there are some uncertainties regarding the project's implementation, which could impact the overall cost-benefit analysis. As such, we will need to be vigilant in monitoring these risks and taking appropriate measures to mitigate them.

Overall, I believe that conducting this cost-benefit analysis was a crucial step in ensuring that the project is completed successfully and with maximum return on investment. It also provides us with a transparent view of the project's financial implications, which is important for our organization's financial planning.

Please let me know if you have any questions or concerns regarding the analysis. I would be more than happy to discuss this with you further and provide any additional support that you may need.

Thank you for your attention to this matter. I look forward to continuing to work with you to ensure the success of this project.

Best regards,

RAHUL PARMAR

[Your Name]

EMAIL 42: REQUESTING CHANGES TO PROJECT SCOPE

By effectively communicating change requests to your boss, you can ensure that the project remains aligned with stakeholder goals and objectives, and ultimately improve project success rates and stakeholder satisfaction. This means that by taking the time to carefully consider and discuss potential changes with your team and stakeholders, and communicating them clearly to your boss, you can set your project up for success and ensure that it meets the needs of all parties involved. So, take the time to consider potential changes to project scope and communicate them effectively to your boss. The value of doing so cannot be overstated.

Sample Email:

Subject Line: Project Scope Change Request for [Project Name]

Dear [Boss's Name],

I hope this email finds you well. I wanted to reach out to you regarding a change request for the scope of [Project Name]. After careful consideration and discussion with the project team and stakeholders, we have identified an opportunity to enhance the project's overall success by implementing a few changes to the project scope.

Specifically, we have identified the need to add an additional feature to the project that will significantly enhance the project's value to our end-users. While this change will require additional resources and time, we strongly believe that it is necessary to meet the project's goals and objectives.

I understand that this change may impact the project timeline and budget. However, we have developed a plan to mitigate any potential negative impact and ensure that the project remains on track. We are confident that with your support, we can successfully implement these changes and achieve our project goals.

I appreciate your time and attention to this matter. Please let me know if you have any questions or concerns regarding this change request. I would be more than happy to discuss this with you further and provide any additional information or clarification that you may need.

Thank you for your continued support and guidance as we work towards the successful completion of [Project Name].

Best regards,
[Your Name]

EMAIL 43: SERVICE LEVEL AGREEMENT DISCUSSION WITH VENDORS

By discussing SLAs with your vendors, you can improve the quality and efficiency of the products and services they provide. This can help you build stronger relationships with your vendors, leading to better collaboration and more successful projects. Additionally, having a clear and effective SLA can streamline your procurement processes, saving you time and resources in the long run.

Don't let SLAs be an afterthought in your vendor relationships. Take the time to discuss them and ensure that you have a strong foundation for success. The benefits are clear: improved vendor relationships and more efficient procurement processes. So, start the discussion today and reap the rewards tomorrow.

Sample Email:

Subject Line: Service Level Agreement Discussion for [Vendor Name]

Dear [Vendor Name],

I hope this email finds you well. I wanted to take a moment to discuss our service level agreement (SLA) for [Vendor Name]. As you know, our company greatly values the relationship we have with your team, and we are committed to ensuring that we have a strong and successful partnership.

To that end, I believe it would be beneficial for us to review our current SLA and discuss any areas where we can make improvements. Specifically, I would like to discuss the timelines and deliverables outlined in the SLA and ensure that they align with our business needs and goals.

Additionally, I would like to discuss the metrics and reporting that are included in the SLA. It is important for us to have clear and measurable goals in place to ensure that we are meeting the agreed-upon service levels.

I understand that this may require some additional time and effort on your part, but I strongly believe that having a clear and effective SLA will greatly benefit both our companies. By improving our vendor relationships and procurement processes, we can ensure that we are both successful in our respective goals.

Please let me know if you have any questions or concerns regarding this discussion. I would be more than happy to set up a meeting or call to discuss this further and work towards a mutually beneficial agreement.

Thank you for your time and consideration, and I look forward to continuing our partnership.

Best regards,
[Your Name]

EMAIL 44: CUSTOMER FEEDBACK REVIEW FOR [PRODUCT NAME]

By reviewing customer feedback and identifying areas for improvement, software project managers can improve product quality and customer satisfaction, which ultimately leads to increased sales and revenue. Listening to customer feedback is crucial to ensuring that the product meets the needs and expectations of its users, and addressing any issues that arise can help to build trust and loyalty with customers. By taking the time to review customer feedback and make improvements based on their suggestions, software project managers can ensure the long-term success of the product and the company as a whole.

Sample Email:

Subject Line: Customer Feedback Review for [Product Name]

Dear [Sales Team Member],

I hope this email finds you well. I wanted to take a moment to discuss our recent customer feedback for [Product Name]. First and foremost, I would like to thank you and the team for your hard work and dedication to ensuring our customers are satisfied with our product.

During the review of the customer feedback, I noticed a few areas where we could make some improvements to the product. Specifically, we received feedback from several customers regarding the user interface, suggesting that it could be made more intuitive and user-friendly. Additionally, some customers have reported issues with certain product features, which we need to investigate further and address.

I understand that addressing these issues may require some additional effort on our part, but I strongly believe that doing so will greatly benefit the product in the long run. By improving the product quality and customer satisfaction, we can increase sales and revenue, as well as improve our brand reputation.

I would like to work closely with you and the sales team to address these issues and ensure that our customers are completely satisfied with the product. Please let me know if you have any suggestions or ideas for how we can improve the product based on the customer feedback.

Thank you again for your hard work and dedication to our customers. I look forward to working with you to ensure the success of [Product Name].

Best regards,
[Your Name]

EMAIL 45: ARCHITECTURE REVIEW FOR [PROJECT NAME]

An architecture review is a critical component of software development that helps to ensure high-quality products and development efficiency. By identifying areas for improvement and simplifying the architecture, developers can reduce complexity and optimize the product to better align with project goals. This not only improves the overall quality of the product but also makes it easier to maintain in the long run. By investing the time and effort into an architecture review, software project managers can ensure that they are delivering a product that meets or exceeds their stakeholders' expectations, leading to increased customer satisfaction and improved project success rates.

Sample Email:

Subject Line: Architecture Review for [Project Name]

Dear [Developer Name],

I hope this email finds you well. I wanted to take a moment to provide feedback on the architecture review for [Project Name]. Firstly, I appreciate your team's hard work on the project, and I believe that we have made great progress so far.

However, during the architecture review, I noticed a few areas where we could make some improvements. Specifically, I think we can simplify the architecture and reduce the complexity in certain areas. This will not only improve the overall quality of the product, but also make it easier to maintain in the long run.

Additionally, I think that we can improve the development efficiency by optimizing the architecture to better align with the project's goals. This will help to ensure that we are meeting the project's requirements and delivering a product that meets or exceeds our stakeholders' expectations.

I understand that these changes may require some additional effort on your part, but I am confident that they will greatly benefit the project. By improving the product quality and development efficiency, we can ensure that we are delivering a product that is of the highest standard.

Please let me know if you have any questions or concerns regarding the feedback provided. I would be more than happy to discuss this with you further and provide any additional support that you may need.

Thank you for your continued dedication and hard work on this project. I look forward to working with you to ensure its success.

Best regards,
[Your Name]

EMAIL 46: PROJECT RISK ASSESSMENT REVIEW FOR [PROJECT NAME]

Identifying and mitigating risks is crucial for the success of any project. Conducting a project risk assessment review allows software project managers to identify potential risks and develop a plan for mitigating them. By proactively managing risks, project success rates are greatly improved, and stakeholder satisfaction is ensured. This email template provides a great example of how to communicate with functional managers regarding project risk assessments and the importance of developing a risk mitigation plan. By using this template, software project managers can streamline their communication, ensure their projects stay on track, and ultimately deliver high-quality results.

Sample Email:

Subject Line: Project Risk Assessment Review for [Project Name]

Dear [Functional Manager Name],

I hope this email finds you well. I am writing to you today to discuss the project risk assessment review for [Project Name]. As you know, identifying and mitigating risks is a critical component of any successful project.

During the review, I noticed a few areas where we may be at risk. Specifically, there are a few dependencies on external vendors that have not yet been fully validated. Additionally, some of the project timelines may be overly optimistic and could result in delays if any issues arise.

I understand that risk management can be a complex and challenging process, but I strongly believe that by identifying and mitigating risks early on, we can greatly improve the success rate of the project and ensure stakeholder satisfaction.

Moving forward, I would like to work with you to develop a plan for mitigating these risks and ensuring that the project stays on track. I believe that by working together, we can proactively manage these risks and ensure the success of the project.

Please let me know if you have any questions or concerns regarding the risk assessment review or the proposed risk mitigation plan. I would be more than happy to discuss this with you further and provide any additional support that you may need.

Thank you for your time and attention to this matter. I look forward to continuing to work with you to ensure the success of the project.

Best regards,
[Your Name]

EMAIL 47: PROJECT TEAM PERFORMANCE METRICS UPDATE

Providing regular performance metrics updates to your boss is essential for the success of your project team. By providing clear and concise updates on key metrics, you can demonstrate the effectiveness and efficiency of your team, as well as your own leadership and management skills. This can help to build trust and confidence with your boss, increase their level of engagement and support, and ensure that your team is well-positioned for continued success. Additionally, by monitoring and reporting on team performance metrics, you can identify areas where improvements can be made, and take proactive steps to address any issues before they become major problems. This ultimately helps to improve team efficiency and productivity, leading to better outcomes for your project and your organization as a whole.

Sample Email:

Subject Line: Project Team Performance Metrics for [Project Name]

Dear [Boss's Name],

I hope this email finds you well. I wanted to provide you with an update on the project team's performance metrics for [Project Name]. As you know, we have been working hard to ensure the success of the project, and I am happy to report that the team is performing at a high level.

Specifically, I would like to highlight a few key metrics that demonstrate the team's efficiency and productivity. First, the team has consistently met or exceeded project milestones, which has helped to ensure that we remain on track to deliver the project on time. Additionally, the team has maintained a high level of code quality and has been proactive in addressing any issues that arise.

Furthermore, I am pleased to report that the team has been working well together and has demonstrated strong collaboration and communication skills. This has helped to ensure that we are able to identify and resolve any issues quickly and efficiently.

I believe that these metrics demonstrate the team's commitment to the success of the project and their ability to work effectively together. I will continue to monitor these metrics closely and provide you with regular updates as the project progresses.

Thank you for your ongoing support of this project and the team. I am confident that with our continued hard work and dedication, we will be able to deliver a successful outcome.

Best regards,
[Your Name]

EMAIL 48: ENHANCING VENDOR RELATIONSHIPS THROUGH VALUABLE FEEDBACK

Providing feedback to vendors is an important part of the software project manager's job, and can have a significant impact on the success of a project. By sharing your insights and suggestions, you can help to improve the product quality and ensure that it meets the needs of your customers.

But the benefits of providing feedback go beyond just improving product quality. By building a strong relationship with your vendors, you can establish a foundation of trust and collaboration that can lead to long-term success. Vendors who feel valued and respected are more likely to go above and beyond to support your projects, and may even offer you exclusive access to new products and services.

So, if you want to enhance your vendor relationships and improve the quality of the products you use, don't hesitate to provide valuable feedback. With the right approach and attitude, you can turn a simple email into a powerful tool for success.

Sample Email:

Subject Line: Product Enhancement Feedback for [Product Name]

Dear [Vendor Name],

I hope this email finds you well. I wanted to take a moment to provide feedback on [Product Name]. Firstly, I want to express my gratitude for the work that you and your team have done so far in developing and delivering this product.

During the usage of the product, I have noticed a few areas where we could enhance the product to better meet the needs of our customers. Specifically, I believe that by adding some new features and functionalities, we can make the product even more user-friendly and efficient.

I wanted to share these ideas with you to get your thoughts and insights. I would greatly appreciate your feedback and suggestions on how we can best implement these enhancements. I believe that by working together, we can create a product that truly meets the needs of our customers and exceeds their expectations.

I value our partnership and the work that we do together, and I believe that this feedback will not only help to improve the quality of the product, but also strengthen our relationship moving forward.

Thank you for your attention to this matter, and I look forward to hearing your thoughts.

Best regards,

EMAIL 49: PRODUCT FEATURE COMPARISON WITH COMPETITORS

By providing your sales team with a detailed feature comparison, you can help them to sell your product more effectively. This can lead to increased sales and revenue for your company. A well-executed feature comparison can help to address customer concerns and objections, and can highlight the unique strengths and value of your product. By demonstrating how your product compares favorably to the competition, you can increase customer confidence and drive more sales. Ultimately, providing a feature comparison is a key component of a successful sales strategy, and can help to ensure the long-term success of your product and your company.

Sample Email:

Subject Line: Product Feature Comparison with Competitors for [Product Name]

Dear [Sales Team],

I hope this email finds you well. As we continue to work towards increasing product sales and revenue for [Product Name], I wanted to provide you with a comparison of our product's features with those of our competitors.

As you know, having a strong understanding of our product's unique selling points and how they compare to the competition is critical to closing deals and driving sales. To help you in this process, I have put together a detailed comparison of our product's features with those of our top competitors. This information can be used to highlight the strengths and unique value of our product, and to address any potential concerns or objections that customers may have.

I believe that this feature comparison will provide you with valuable insights and tools to help you sell our product more effectively. By emphasizing the unique strengths of our product and demonstrating how it compares favorably to the competition, we can increase customer confidence and drive more sales.

Please let me know if you have any questions or if there is anything else I can do to support you in your sales efforts. I am always available to help in any way that I can.

Thank you for your continued dedication to driving sales for [Product Name]. Together, we can achieve great success.

Best regards,
[Your Name]

EMAIL 50: TECHNICAL ROADMAP FOR [PROJECT NAME]

A well-defined technical roadmap is critical for the success of any software development project. It provides a clear vision of the project goals, outlines the technical specifications and requirements for each stage of the project, and ensures that the development team is aligned and working towards a common goal. A technical roadmap also enables software project managers to incorporate agile methodologies into the development process, resulting in improved development efficiency and quality. By breaking down the project into smaller, more manageable components, teams can ensure that each stage of the development process is completed to the highest standards. In this email, we provide a sample message that software project managers can use to communicate with their development team regarding the technical roadmap for their project, including the importance of incorporating agile methodologies into the roadmap.

Sample Email:

Subject Line: Technical Roadmap for [Project Name]

Dear [Developer Name],

I hope this email finds you well. I wanted to reach out regarding the technical roadmap for [Project Name]. As you know, a technical roadmap is an essential component of any successful project, as it helps to ensure that the development team is aligned and working towards a common goal.

To that end, I wanted to share my vision for the technical roadmap and get your input and feedback. Specifically, I think that we should focus on developing a roadmap that outlines the technical specifications and requirements for each stage of the project. This will help to ensure that we are all on the same page and working towards the same goals.

Additionally, I think that we should consider incorporating agile methodologies into the technical roadmap, as this can help to improve development efficiency and quality. By breaking down the project into smaller, more manageable components, we can ensure that each stage of the development process is completed to the highest standards.

I would love to hear your thoughts on this and get your feedback on how we can create the most effective technical roadmap for [Project Name]. Please let me know if you have any questions or concerns regarding this.

Thank you for your hard work and dedication to this project. I look forward to continuing to work with you to ensure its success.

Best regards,
[Your Name]

EMAIL 51: PROJECT QUALITY METRICS REVIEW

Regular review of project quality metrics is essential for software project managers to identify areas for improvement and ensure high-quality product delivery. By analyzing metrics such as testing efficiency and documentation quality, project managers can make data-driven decisions to improve product quality and enhance customer satisfaction. This email provides a perfect example of how project managers can collaborate with functional managers to review quality metrics and identify areas for improvement. By working together to prioritize quality, project managers can deliver products that meet the highest standards and exceed customer expectations.

Sample Email:

Subject Line: Project Quality Metrics Review for [Project Name]

Dear [Functional Manager Name],

I hope this email finds you well. I wanted to take a moment to discuss the quality metrics for [Project Name]. As the software project manager, it is essential for me to review these metrics regularly to ensure that we are meeting the highest standards and delivering the best possible product.

During my review, I noticed a few areas where we could make some improvements to further enhance the quality of the project. Specifically, I think we could focus on improving the efficiency of our testing processes, and perhaps look into some additional testing tools or techniques. Additionally, I noticed that we could improve our documentation to provide better clarity and support for our users.

By focusing on these areas, we can improve the overall quality of the project, which will directly impact customer satisfaction. By delivering a high-quality product, we can ensure that our users have a positive experience and are more likely to recommend our product to others.

I wanted to discuss these areas with you to ensure that we are all on the same page and working towards the same goals. Please let me know if you have any feedback or suggestions on how we can improve these areas, or if you have any questions regarding the quality metrics review.

Thank you for your time and attention to this matter. I look forward to working with you to continue to improve the quality of our project.

Best regards,
[Your Name]

EMAIL 52: PROJECT COMMUNICATION PLAN FOR [PROJECT NAME]

Effective communication is critical to the success of any project, and a well-crafted project communication plan can make all the difference. By taking the time to develop and communicate a detailed plan, project managers can ensure that all stakeholders are kept informed, engaged, and up-to-date throughout the project. This helps to build trust and confidence among stakeholders, reduce the risk of misunderstandings and conflicts, and ultimately lead to a successful project outcome. A project communication plan is an investment in the success of your project, and it is essential for any project manager looking to improve their communication skills and streamline their daily work. With the right communication plan in place, you can be confident that your project is on the path to success.

Sample Email:

Subject Line: Project Communication Plan for [Project Name]

Dear [Boss's Name],

I hope this email finds you well. I wanted to provide an update on the progress of [Project Name] and share with you the communication plan that we have developed for the project.

As we discussed previously, clear communication and stakeholder engagement are essential for the success of any project. In light of this, we have developed a detailed project communication plan that outlines the communication channels, frequency, and messaging for all project stakeholders.

Our communication plan includes regular status updates, progress reports, and stakeholder meetings to ensure that everyone is up-to-date and informed about the project's progress. Additionally, we have identified key stakeholders and developed specific messaging for each group to ensure that their needs and concerns are addressed.

By implementing this communication plan, we can ensure that all stakeholders are kept informed and engaged throughout the project. This will help to improve communication and visibility, increase stakeholder satisfaction, and ultimately lead to a successful project outcome.

I would be happy to provide you with a copy of the project communication plan and answer any questions you may have. Please let me know if this would be helpful.

Thank you for your support and guidance on this project. I look forward to continuing to work with you to ensure its success.

Best regards,
[Your Name]

EMAIL 53: SHARING A PRODUCT IMPROVEMENT ROADMAP WITH VENDORS

By sharing your product improvement roadmap with vendors, you not only demonstrate a commitment to collaboration and transparency, but you also open the door to valuable feedback and insight from your vendors. This collaboration can lead to stronger relationships and better communication between the two parties, which can greatly benefit your product development efforts.

Furthermore, involving vendors in the product improvement process can lead to improved product quality. Vendors often have valuable expertise and insights into their respective areas of the product, which can be leveraged to drive improvements and optimize performance. By working together, you can create a product that meets the needs of your customers and exceeds their expectations.

Sample Email:

Subject Line: Product Improvement Roadmap for [Product Name]

Dear [Vendor Name],

I hope this email finds you well. I wanted to take a moment to discuss our plans for improving [Product Name]. As you know, we value your contributions to the product and are committed to working closely with you to ensure its success.

To that end, I wanted to share our product improvement roadmap with you. We have identified several areas where we believe the product can be improved, such as increasing its performance, enhancing its user interface, and adding new features. We believe that these improvements will greatly benefit our customers and help us to maintain a competitive edge in the market.

We would greatly appreciate your input and collaboration in this process. Specifically, we would like to work with you to identify the best ways to implement these improvements and to ensure that they align with your development roadmap for the product.

We believe that by working together, we can create a product that meets the needs of our customers and exceeds their expectations. We also believe that this collaboration will lead to improved vendor relationships and product quality, which will benefit us both in the long run.

Thank you for your time and attention to this matter. I look forward to hearing your thoughts on the product improvement roadmap and working together to bring these improvements to fruition.

Best regards,

[Your Name]

EMAIL 54: PRODUCT PRICING STRATEGY UPDATE

A carefully considered and well-implemented pricing strategy can have a significant impact on the success of a product. By increasing prices slightly while remaining competitive, you can increase revenue and attract customers who value the unique features and benefits of your product. Communicating this strategy effectively to your sales team and customers is key to managing the transition and ensuring a smooth rollout. By providing the right information and support, you can build trust and confidence with your stakeholders and achieve your sales goals.

Sample Email:

Subject Line: Product Pricing Strategy Update for [Product Name]

Dear [Sales Team],

I hope this email finds you well. I wanted to take a moment to update you on the pricing strategy for our [Product Name]. As you know, we have been working hard to develop a pricing strategy that maximizes revenue while remaining competitive in the market.

After careful consideration and analysis, we have decided to implement a new pricing strategy for [Product Name]. This strategy will involve a slight increase in the price of the product, but we are confident that it will lead to increased sales and revenue.

Our research has shown that customers are willing to pay a premium for the features and benefits provided by [Product Name], and we believe that this new pricing strategy will help to capitalize on this trend. We will also be providing additional marketing support to help communicate the value proposition of [Product Name] to customers.

I understand that this may be a change from what we have previously communicated to customers, and I want to assure you that we have developed a plan to manage this transition smoothly. We will be communicating the new pricing strategy to customers through various channels, and we will work closely with you to ensure that you have the information and support that you need to answer any questions or concerns that customers may have.

I am confident that this new pricing strategy will help us to increase sales and revenue for [Product Name], and I look forward to working with you to make it a success.

If you have any questions or concerns regarding this update, please do not hesitate to reach out to me. I am always here to support you in any way that I can.

Best regards,
[Your Name]

EMAIL 55: EFFECTIVE DEPENDENCY MANAGEMENT FOR SUCCESSFUL PROJECTS

Effective dependency management provides numerous benefits for software project managers. It enables better resource allocation, reduces project risks, and improves communication between team members. By managing dependencies proactively, software project managers can minimize delays, ensure timely delivery, and ensure high-quality code. Effective dependency management also allows software project managers to stay on top of project progress, communicate effectively with stakeholders, and optimize project timelines. In short, effective dependency management is critical for achieving success in software projects.

Sample Email:

Subject Line: Dependency Management Plan for [Project Name]

Dear [Developer Name],

I hope this email finds you well. I wanted to take a moment to discuss our dependency management plan for [Project Name]. As you know, effective management of project dependencies is critical to the success of any project.

We have identified a few dependencies that require our attention, and I would like to work with you to develop a plan to manage them effectively. By doing so, we can ensure that the project is completed on time and to the highest standards.

To start, I would like to schedule a meeting to discuss the dependencies in more detail and to identify any potential risks or issues. During this meeting, we can also outline a plan to manage the dependencies, including assigning responsibilities and setting timelines.

I understand that managing dependencies can be a complex and time-consuming process, but I believe that it is essential for improving development efficiency and quality. By addressing dependencies proactively, we can minimize delays and ensure that the project is delivered on time and to the highest standards.

Please let me know your availability to schedule this meeting, and if you have any questions or concerns, please don't hesitate to reach out to me. I appreciate your hard work and dedication to this project and look forward to continuing to work with you to ensure its success.

Best regards,
[Your Name]

EMAIL 56: PROJECT STAKEHOLDER ANALYSIS

Conducting a stakeholder analysis is a critical component of project management that can significantly improve project success rates and stakeholder satisfaction. By gathering information about the stakeholders, their interests, and their expectations, project managers can tailor their project strategies to better meet stakeholder needs. This not only leads to increased stakeholder satisfaction but can also help to identify potential risks and opportunities for the project. In short, conducting a stakeholder analysis is a vital tool for project managers looking to achieve success in their projects and build strong relationships with their stakeholders.

Sample Email:

Subject Line: Project Stakeholder Analysis for [Project Name]

Dear [Functional Manager Name],

I hope this email finds you well. I wanted to take a moment to discuss the importance of conducting a stakeholder analysis for [Project Name]. As you are aware, identifying and understanding the needs of our project stakeholders is critical to the success of the project.

To ensure that we are meeting the expectations and needs of our stakeholders, I am initiating a stakeholder analysis for the project. This analysis will involve gathering information about the stakeholders, their interests, and their expectations for the project.

By conducting this analysis, we will gain a better understanding of the project stakeholders and their needs. This will enable us to tailor our project strategy to better meet their expectations, ultimately leading to increased stakeholder satisfaction and improved project success rates.

I would like to request your assistance in this effort. Specifically, I would appreciate your help in identifying the key stakeholders for the project and any insights you may have into their interests and expectations. Your input will be critical to ensuring the success of this analysis and, ultimately, the success of the project.

Thank you in advance for your support and cooperation in this effort. I look forward to working with you to ensure the success of [Project Name].

Best regards,
[Your Name]

EMAIL 57: IMPROVING PROJECT SUCCESS RATES WITH A BENEFITS REALIZATION PLAN

A benefits realization plan is a critical component of successful project management. By clearly outlining the benefits that a project is expected to deliver, the metrics that will be used to measure progress, and the actions that will be taken to ensure that those benefits are realized, project managers can increase the likelihood of project success and stakeholder satisfaction. The plan serves as a roadmap for the project and provides a framework for decision-making and resource allocation. With a benefits realization plan in place, project managers can demonstrate their commitment to delivering value and ensure that everyone is aligned and working towards a common goal. By taking the time to develop and communicate a benefits realization plan, project managers can improve their communication skills, streamline their daily work, and achieve success in their projects.

Sample Email:

Subject Line: Project Benefits Realization Plan for [Project Name]

Dear [Boss Name],

I hope this email finds you well. I wanted to take a moment to provide an update on the benefits realization plan for [Project Name]. As we move forward with the project, it's important that we have a clear plan in place to ensure that we realize the full benefits of the project for the company and our stakeholders.

To that end, I have been working with the project team to develop a benefits realization plan that outlines the specific benefits that we expect to achieve from the project, the metrics that we will use to measure these benefits, and the actions that we will take to ensure that we realize these benefits.

The benefits that we expect to achieve from the project include [list of benefits], and we have identified specific metrics that we will use to measure our progress towards achieving these benefits. In addition, we have outlined a series of actions that we will take to ensure that we realize these benefits, including [list of actions].

I believe that having a clear benefits realization plan in place will greatly improve the success of the project and increase stakeholder satisfaction. By communicating this plan to our stakeholders, we can demonstrate our commitment to achieving the benefits that we have promised and ensure that everyone is aligned and working towards a common goal.

Please let me know if you have any questions or concerns regarding the benefits realization plan. I would be more than happy to discuss this with you further and provide any additional information that you may need.

Thank you for your continued support of this project.

Best regards,
[Your Name]

EMAIL 58: PRODUCT ROADMAP REVIEW

Reviewing vendor product roadmaps is a critical component of successful software project management. By reviewing vendor product roadmaps, software project managers can ensure that their development plans are aligned with their vendor's goals and objectives. This, in turn, can help to improve the overall quality of the product and strengthen vendor relationships. By staying up-to-date on vendor product roadmaps and any changes or updates, software project managers can make more informed decisions and ensure that their projects are completed on time and to the highest standards. Ultimately, by investing time in reviewing vendor product roadmaps, software project managers can achieve greater success in their projects and build stronger partnerships with their vendors.

Sample Email:

Subject Line: Product Roadmap Review for [Product Name]

Dear [Vendor Name],

I hope this email finds you well. As the software project manager for [Product Name], I wanted to take a moment to touch base with you regarding your product roadmap. We have always valued the partnership that we have with your company and would like to ensure that our objectives are aligned.

As we move forward with the development of [Product Name], it is important that we review and discuss any changes or updates to the product roadmap. I would appreciate it if you could provide me with a copy of your current roadmap and any updates or changes that you are planning to make in the near future.

By reviewing your product roadmap, we can ensure that our product development plans are aligned with your company's goals and objectives. This, in turn, will improve the overall quality of the product and strengthen our vendor relationship.

Thank you for your cooperation and support. I look forward to hearing back from you soon.

Best regards,
[Your Name]

EMAIL 59: SALES PIPELINE REVIEW FOR [PRODUCT NAME]

The sales pipeline is a critical component of any business, and as a software project manager, it's important to review it regularly to ensure that we are maximizing our sales potential. By conducting a sales pipeline review for [Product Name], we can identify potential opportunities to increase product sales and revenue. This review allows us to target key market segments and develop targeted marketing materials to increase product awareness among potential customers. By using this email template, software project managers can provide valuable feedback and insights to the sales team, ensuring that everyone is working together to achieve the same goal. By improving the sales pipeline, we can increase product sales and revenue, which is essential for the long-term success of any business.

Sample Email:

Subject Line: Sales Pipeline Review for [Product Name]

Dear [Sales Team],

I hope this email finds you well. I wanted to touch base with you regarding the sales pipeline for [Product Name]. As the software project manager, it's important for me to review the pipeline and identify potential opportunities for increased product sales and revenue.

Based on my review, I believe there are a few areas where we could focus our efforts to improve the sales pipeline. Specifically, I think we could target a few key market segments where the product has shown particular strength. Additionally, we could work to develop some targeted marketing materials to increase product awareness among potential customers.

I would also like to encourage everyone on the sales team to continue to provide feedback and insights on the sales pipeline. Your input is invaluable in identifying areas for improvement and developing strategies to increase product sales.

Please let me know if you have any questions or concerns regarding the sales pipeline review. I would be more than happy to discuss this with you further and provide any additional support that you may need.

Thank you for your hard work and dedication to the success of [Product Name]. I look forward to continuing to work with you to increase sales and revenue.

Best regards,
[Your Name]

EMAIL 60: CODE REFACTORING PLAN FOR [PROJECT NAME]

Code refactoring is an essential process for software projects that can significantly improve code quality and development efficiency. By refactoring code, we can reduce technical debt, make future development easier, and ensure that the project is completed on time and to the highest standards. A well-planned and prioritized code refactoring plan can help software project managers to streamline the development process and reduce the risk of bugs. This can lead to improved project success rates and stakeholder satisfaction. By implementing a code refactoring plan, software project managers can set their projects up for long-term success and ensure the delivery of high-quality products.

Sample Email:

Subject Line: Code Refactoring Plan for [Project Name]

Dear [Developer Name],

I hope this email finds you well. As we continue to make progress on [Project Name], I wanted to discuss the importance of code refactoring and share with you a plan that I believe will greatly benefit the project.

As you know, code refactoring is the process of improving the internal structure of code without changing its external functionality. By doing so, we can improve code quality, reduce technical debt, and make development more efficient.

With that in mind, I would like to propose a plan for code refactoring on [Project Name]. I have identified several areas where code refactoring would be most beneficial, and I would like to prioritize these tasks in order of importance.

I understand that code refactoring can be time-consuming and may require additional effort, but I strongly believe that it will greatly benefit the project in the long run. By improving the code quality and development efficiency, we can reduce the risk of bugs, make future development easier, and ensure that the project is completed on time and to the highest standards.

I would appreciate your feedback on the proposed plan and any additional insights you may have. Together, I believe we can make significant improvements to the project and continue to exceed our goals.

Thank you for your hard work and dedication to this project. I look forward to continuing to work with you to ensure its success.

Best regards,
[Your Name]

EMAIL 61: CONDUCTING A PROJECT FEASIBILITY STUDY

A project feasibility study is an essential component of successful project management. By conducting a feasibility study, software project managers can identify potential risks, challenges, and opportunities that may impact the project's success. This enables them to make informed decisions and take the necessary steps to ensure that the project is completed on time, within budget, and to the highest quality standards.

Moreover, a feasibility study helps to align project goals with stakeholder expectations and ensures that the project is feasible in terms of technical, financial, and operational requirements. It provides a clear understanding of the project scope, timeline, and resource requirements, which is crucial for effective project planning and management.

A well-executed feasibility study can greatly improve project success rates and stakeholder satisfaction by minimizing risks and uncertainties, increasing transparency, and enhancing communication among project stakeholders. It enables software project managers to identify potential issues early on and take proactive measures to mitigate them, which ultimately leads to better project outcomes.

Sample Email:

Subject Line: Project Feasibility Study for [Project Name]

Dear [Functional Manager Name],

I hope this email finds you well. I wanted to take a moment to discuss the feasibility study for [Project Name] that we recently conducted. Firstly, I would like to express my gratitude for your cooperation and contributions to the study. Your valuable insights and recommendations have been extremely helpful in shaping the direction of the project.

Based on the findings of the feasibility study, it is clear that [Project Name] is a viable project and has the potential to be successful. However, there were a few areas that we identified that require further attention in order to ensure the project's success.

Specifically, we need to focus on improving the project's timeline and ensuring that we have the necessary resources in place to complete the project on time. Additionally, we need to closely monitor the project's budget and make sure that we are making efficient use of our resources.

I am confident that with your continued support and guidance, we can address these issues and successfully complete the project. By conducting a feasibility study and taking these steps, we can greatly improve the project's success rates and stakeholder satisfaction.

Thank you again for your contributions to the feasibility study. Please let me know if you have any questions or concerns, or if there is anything else I can do to support you.

Best regards,
[Your Name]

EMAIL 62: CONDUCTING A POST-IMPLEMENTATION REVIEW FOR PROJECT SUCCESS

Conducting a post-implementation review for software projects is critical for project success and stakeholder satisfaction. It allows project managers to assess the project's success rates against the initial objectives and goals, identify any areas of improvement, and gather feedback from stakeholders. By reflecting on the project outcomes and identifying any lessons learned, project managers can improve their processes and practices for future projects. Additionally, conducting a post-implementation review demonstrates a commitment to quality and continuous improvement, which can enhance the reputation of the organization and build trust with stakeholders. Overall, conducting a post-implementation review is an essential step in ensuring the success of software projects and delivering value to stakeholders.

Sample Email:

Subject Line: Project Post-Implementation Review for [Project Name]

Dear [Boss's Name],

I hope this email finds you well. I wanted to discuss with you the importance of conducting a post-implementation review for [Project Name]. As you know, the project has now been completed and delivered to the stakeholders, but it is important for us to conduct a review to ensure its success.

The post-implementation review will allow us to assess the project's success against the initial objectives and goals. We can evaluate the project outcomes, identify any areas of improvement, and gather feedback from the stakeholders. Additionally, we can use the review to identify any lessons learned, which can be applied to future projects.

By conducting this review, we can ensure that the project's success rates are improved and that the stakeholders are satisfied with the project outcomes. It is important that we take the time to reflect on the project and its outcomes to ensure that we continue to improve our processes and practices.

I propose that we schedule the review for next week, and I will prepare a report outlining the project outcomes and recommendations for improvement. Please let me know if you have any additional thoughts or concerns regarding the post-implementation review.

Thank you for your time and attention to this matter. I look forward to your response.

Best regards,
[Your Name]

EMAIL 63: PROVIDING VENDOR FEEDBACK FOR PRODUCT TESTING

Providing feedback to vendors on product testing is an essential part of the software development process. By doing so, you can ensure that any issues are identified and addressed before the product is released to customers. This not only improves the quality of the product but also enhances your vendor relationships by showing them that you are invested in their success. By taking the time to provide feedback and work collaboratively with vendors, you can ensure that your partnership is strong and that you can deliver the best possible product to your customers.

Sample Email:

Subject Line: Product Testing Feedback for [Product Name]

Dear [Vendor Name],

I hope this email finds you well. I wanted to take a moment to provide some feedback on the product testing for [Product Name]. Firstly, I wanted to thank you and your team for your hard work and dedication to ensuring the quality of the product.

During the testing process, our team identified a few areas where we think the product could be improved. Specifically, we noticed a few issues with the user interface that we believe could be made more intuitive and user-friendly. Additionally, there were a few areas where the product could be made more scalable and flexible to accommodate different use cases.

I understand that these changes may require some additional effort on your part, but I strongly believe that they will greatly benefit the product and our customers in the long run. By improving the product quality and addressing any issues, we can ensure that our customers are satisfied and that our partnership continues to be successful.

Please let me know if you have any questions or concerns regarding the feedback provided. I would be more than happy to discuss this with you further and provide any additional support that you may need.

Once again, thank you for your hard work and dedication to this product. I look forward to continuing our partnership and working together to deliver the best possible product to our customers.

Best regards,
[Your Name]

EMAIL 64: CUSTOMIZING PRODUCT DEMOS FOR INCREASED SALES

Value: Customizing product demos can significantly increase sales by tailoring them to meet the specific needs and preferences of potential customers. By showcasing the features and benefits of the product that are most relevant to the customer's business, we can increase their interest in the product and increase the likelihood of converting them into actual customers. Customizing the product demo also shows that we understand and care about their needs, which can build trust and improve our overall relationship with the customer. Overall, customization is an important step in our sales strategy that can result in increased product sales and revenue.

Sample Email:

Subject Line: Customization of [Product Name] Demo for Sales Team

Dear [Sales Team Name],

I hope this email finds you well. I wanted to discuss the customization of the [Product Name] demo for our sales team. As you know, the demo is a key tool for our team to showcase the features and benefits of our product to potential customers. To maximize the effectiveness of the demo, I strongly believe that we should customize it for the specific needs and preferences of our customers.

To achieve this, I would like to request your input on how we can customize the demo to better meet the needs of your customers. This may include tailoring the demo to showcase specific features that are of particular interest to your customers, or highlighting certain benefits that may be most relevant to their business.

By customizing the demo in this way, we can increase the likelihood of converting potential customers into actual customers, thereby increasing product sales and revenue. I believe that this is an important step in our overall sales strategy, and I look forward to working with you to ensure its success.

Please let me know your thoughts on this matter, and if you have any suggestions on how we can improve the demo customization process. I am available to discuss this further at your convenience.

Thank you for your time and efforts in this regard. I appreciate your partnership and support in driving the success of our product.

Best regards,
[Your Name]

EMAIL 65: IMPROVING PROJECT DOCUMENTATION FOR BETTER DEVELOPMENT EFFICIENCY

Clear and concise project documentation is crucial for the success of any software project. By improving project documentation, software project managers can ensure that all team members and stakeholders are on the same page and that the project is completed on time and to the highest standards. Detailed project documentation helps in identifying areas of improvement, reduces the chances of errors, and streamlines communication between team members. With a clear understanding of the project requirements and scope, developers can work more efficiently, saving time and resources. Improved project documentation also helps in enhancing the overall product quality, which is vital for customer satisfaction and business success. By investing in better project documentation, software project managers can optimize development efficiency, reduce errors, and improve product quality, ultimately leading to better business outcomes.

Sample Email:

Subject Line: Project Documentation Review for [Project Name]

Dear [Developer Name],

I hope this email finds you well. I wanted to take a moment to review the project documentation for [Project Name]. Firstly, I want to thank you and the team for the hard work and dedication that has been put into this project. Your contributions are greatly appreciated.

During my review of the project documentation, I noticed a few areas where we could make some improvements. Specifically, I think we could provide more detailed information about the project requirements and scope, as well as the project timeline and milestones. I also noticed that there were some inconsistencies in the documentation, which could be confusing for team members and stakeholders.

As you know, having clear and concise project documentation is crucial for ensuring that the project is completed on time and to the highest standards. By improving the documentation, we can improve development efficiency and product quality, while also ensuring that all team members and stakeholders are on the same page.

I understand that reviewing and updating the documentation may require additional effort on your part, but I strongly believe that it will greatly benefit the project in the long run. I would like to work with you and the team to make the necessary improvements and ensure that the project documentation accurately reflects the project scope and requirements.

Please let me know if you have any questions or concerns regarding the feedback provided. I would be more than happy to discuss this with you further and provide any additional support that you may need.

Thank you again for your hard work and dedication to this project. I look forward to continuing to work with you to ensure its success.

Best regards,
[Your Name]

EMAIL 66: PROJECT COMMUNICATION WITH A COMMUNICATION AUDIT

Effective communication is critical to the success of any project. Without clear and structured communication between teams and stakeholders, projects can quickly fall behind schedule, miss key milestones, and fail to meet expectations. That's why conducting a communication audit is so important. By evaluating your project's communication practices, you can identify areas for improvement, streamline communication, and ensure that everyone is working towards the same goals. A communication audit can help you uncover issues that may be preventing effective communication, such as unclear roles and responsibilities, lack of transparency, or misalignment between teams. By addressing these issues, you can improve communication and visibility, increase stakeholder satisfaction, and ultimately ensure the success of your project. So, if you're looking to take your project communication to the next level, consider conducting a communication audit today.

Sample Email:

Subject Line: Project Communication Audit for [Project Name]

Dear [Functional Manager Name],

I hope this email finds you well. I wanted to touch base with you regarding the project communication for [Project Name]. As the software project manager, it's important for me to ensure that communication between teams and stakeholders is efficient and effective.

To that end, I've conducted a communication audit for the project, and I wanted to share my findings with you. Overall, I believe that we have a solid foundation in place, but there are a few areas where we can make some improvements.

Specifically, I think we can benefit from more regular check-ins with stakeholders to keep them informed of our progress. Additionally, we could benefit from more structured communication between teams to ensure that everyone is aligned and working towards the same goals.

I understand that this may require some additional effort on our part, but I strongly believe that it will be worth it in the long run. By improving our communication and visibility, we can ensure that the project is completed on time and to the highest standards.

Please let me know if you have any questions or concerns regarding the audit findings. I would be more than happy to discuss this with you further and provide any additional support that you may need.

Thank you for your time and attention to this matter. I look forward to continuing to work with you to ensure the success of [Project Name].

Best regards,
[Your Name]

EMAIL 67: REVIEWING PROJECT RESOURCE UTILIZATION FOR IMPROVED FINANCIAL PLANNING

By optimizing resource utilization, software project managers can reduce unnecessary costs and improve financial planning and transparency. This not only benefits the project and company as a whole but also ensures that resources are allocated effectively and efficiently. With improved financial planning, software project managers can invest savings in other critical areas of the project, such as innovation and development, to drive further success.

In this particular email, the software project manager provides their boss with an update on the project's resource utilization and identifies potential areas for optimization. By discussing these findings with their boss and implementing a plan to address inefficiencies, the project manager can significantly improve the project's financial performance and ensure its long-term success.

Sample Email:

Subject Line: Project Resource Utilization Review for [Project Name]

Dear [Boss's Name],

I hope this email finds you well. I wanted to provide an update on the resource utilization for [Project Name]. As you know, effective resource utilization is critical to the success of the project and the company as a whole. With that in mind, I conducted a thorough review of the project's resource utilization and identified some potential areas where we can optimize our usage.

Specifically, I found that we have been using some resources inefficiently, which has resulted in higher costs than necessary. By optimizing our resource utilization, we can reduce these costs and improve our financial planning and transparency. This will enable us to invest those savings in other critical areas of the project.

I have developed a plan to address these areas of inefficiency, which I would like to discuss with you in more detail during our next meeting. I believe that by making these changes, we can significantly improve the project's financial performance and help to ensure its long-term success.

Thank you for your attention to this matter. I look forward to discussing this with you further.

Best regards,
[Your Name]

EMAIL 68: REQUESTING VENDOR CONTRACT AMENDMENTS

Requesting vendor contract amendments can have significant value for your project and your organization. By ensuring that the contract aligns with your project requirements and timelines, you can avoid potential delays or issues down the road. Additionally, by communicating your needs and concerns with your vendor in a clear and professional manner, you can improve your vendor relationships and procurement processes overall.

The key to success in this situation is effective communication. By using a template like the one provided, you can ensure that your message is clear, concise, and professional. Additionally, by explaining the reasons behind the requested amendments and being open to feedback and guidance from your vendor, you can establish a positive and collaborative relationship that benefits both parties.

Sample Email:

Subject Line: Vendor Contract Amendment Request for [Vendor Name]

Dear [Vendor Contact Name],

I hope this email finds you well. I wanted to discuss a few amendments to the current vendor contract between [Vendor Name] and [Company Name]. As you are aware, we have had a long and successful relationship, and we greatly value the work that your team has done for us.

However, as our project requirements have evolved, we believe that it is necessary to request a few amendments to the current contract. Specifically, we would like to discuss the following changes:

Change in delivery timelines for specific milestones
Change in payment terms and schedules
Addition of specific service level agreements (SLAs) related to the project
We believe that these changes will benefit both parties and help to ensure the continued success of our project. We value your expertise and would appreciate your feedback and guidance regarding these changes.

Please let me know if you have any questions or concerns regarding the amendments requested. I would be more than happy to discuss this with you further and provide any additional support that you may need.

Thank you for your continued partnership and support. We look forward to continuing to work with you to achieve our project goals.

Best regards,
[Your Name]

EMAIL 69: PRIORITIZING PRODUCT FEATURE REQUESTS

By prioritizing product feature requests, you can optimize your development efforts and ensure that you are delivering features that meet the needs of your customers. This can lead to increased customer satisfaction, improved product quality, and ultimately, increased sales and revenue.

In addition, prioritizing feature requests can also help you manage your resources more effectively. By focusing on the features that have the greatest potential to drive sales and revenue, you can ensure that you are allocating your resources in the most efficient and effective way possible.

Sample Email:

Subject Line: Prioritizing Product Feature Requests for [Product Name]

Dear [Sales Team Member],

I hope this email finds you well. As we continue to develop [Product Name], I wanted to take a moment to discuss the prioritization of product feature requests from the sales team.

We appreciate all of the feedback and suggestions that have been provided thus far, and we understand that each request has the potential to drive increased product sales and revenue. However, we also need to ensure that we are prioritizing these requests in a way that aligns with our overall goals and objectives for the product.

To that end, I would like to request your assistance in prioritizing the product feature requests that have been submitted. Specifically, I would like to ask you to rank these requests based on the following criteria:

Potential impact on product sales and revenue
Alignment with overall product goals and objectives
Feasibility for implementation within a reasonable timeframe
By taking these criteria into consideration, we can ensure that we are prioritizing the product feature requests that have the greatest potential to drive increased product sales and revenue while also aligning with our overall goals and objectives for the product.

I appreciate your assistance with this, and I am confident that by working together, we can continue to make [Product Name] a success.

Please let me know if you have any questions or concerns regarding this request. I would be more than happy to discuss this with you further.

Best regards,
[Your Name]

EMAIL 70: NEED FOR EFFECTIVE PROJECT DEPLOYMENT PLANNING

Effective project deployment planning is a critical component of successful software projects. Without a well-planned and executed deployment plan, there can be delays, increased costs, and decreased customer satisfaction. By ensuring that there is a clear plan in place, software project managers can not only improve the overall quality of the product but also increase customer satisfaction, which is critical to the success of any software project. Effective project deployment planning can also help identify potential risks and challenges, which can be addressed before they become bigger problems. This can ultimately save time, money, and resources, and lead to a successful project outcome. By taking the time to plan and manage project deployments, software project managers can ensure the long-term success of their projects and their companies.

Sample Email:

Subject Line: Project Deployment Plan for [Project Name]

Dear [Developer Name],

I hope this email finds you well. I wanted to take a moment to discuss the project deployment plan for [Project Name]. As we near the completion of the project, it is essential that we have a clear plan in place for the deployment process.

I am writing to request your input on the deployment plan for the project. Specifically, I would like to discuss the timeline for deployment, the necessary steps involved in the process, and any potential challenges that we may face.

I understand that the deployment process can be complex and time-consuming, but I strongly believe that by having a well-planned and executed deployment plan, we can improve the overall product quality and customer satisfaction.

As a software project manager, it is my responsibility to ensure that the deployment process is planned and executed effectively. I am committed to working closely with you and the rest of the team to make this happen.

Please let me know if you have any thoughts or ideas regarding the deployment plan for the project. I would be happy to set up a meeting to discuss this further and ensure that we have a plan that is both effective and efficient.

Thank you for your hard work and dedication to this project. I look forward to working with you to ensure its successful deployment.

Best regards,

[Your Name]

EMAIL 71: PROJECT SCHEDULE COMPRESSION PLAN

Time is a critical component of any software project. Delays in project schedules can lead to missed deadlines, dissatisfied stakeholders, and increased costs. As a software project manager, it is important to have a plan in place to compress project schedules when necessary. By creating a project schedule compression plan, you can act quickly to address any potential delays and ensure that the project is completed on time and to the highest standards. This not only improves project timelines and success rates but also demonstrates your ability to be proactive and responsive to unforeseen circumstances. With "The Ultimate Resource for Software Project Managers: 100 Email Templates for Every Project Scenario," you'll have the perfect words to communicate your plan effectively and achieve success in your projects.

Sample Email:

Subject Line: Project Schedule Compression Plan for [Project Name]

Dear [Functional Manager Name],

I hope this email finds you well. I wanted to discuss the project schedule for [Project Name] and explore options for compressing the timeline, if necessary.

As you are aware, the project schedule is a critical component of the project management plan. It outlines the tasks, dependencies, and deadlines required to complete the project successfully. However, in some cases, unforeseen circumstances can arise, leading to schedule delays and potential project setbacks.

To mitigate the risks associated with potential schedule delays, I have created a project schedule compression plan. This plan outlines various strategies that we can use to accelerate the project timeline if necessary, such as implementing overlapping activities or re-sequencing tasks.

By having this plan in place, we can act quickly to address any issues that may arise, and ensure that the project is completed on time and to the highest standards. I believe that this will greatly improve our project timelines and success rates.

I would love to discuss this plan with you in more detail and receive your input. Please let me know if you have any questions or concerns regarding this matter.

Thank you for your time and attention to this matter. I look forward to hearing back from you.

Best regards,
[Your Name]

EMAIL 72: REVIEWING PROJECT SUCCESS CRITERIA WITH BOSS

By reviewing project success criteria with your boss, you can ensure that your project aligns with stakeholder expectations and achieve project success. This process can help you identify potential risks or issues early on and take corrective action as needed. Additionally, it can help you create a shared understanding of what constitutes success, which can improve stakeholder satisfaction and project outcomes. Taking the time to review project success criteria with your boss is a critical step in ensuring the success of your project and building strong relationships with stakeholders.

Sample Email:

Subject Line: Project Success Criteria Review for [Project Name]

Dear [Boss Name],

I hope this email finds you well. As the software project manager for [Project Name], I wanted to take a moment to review the project success criteria with you to ensure that we are aligned with stakeholder expectations.

Based on our discussions with stakeholders, I believe the success criteria should focus on the following key areas: meeting project deadlines, delivering high-quality code, and ensuring that the project is within budget. However, I wanted to confirm with you if there are any additional criteria or changes that we should consider.

By reviewing and aligning the project success criteria, we can ensure that the project is completed successfully and that stakeholder satisfaction is achieved. It also helps us to identify potential risks or issues early on and take corrective action as needed.

Please let me know if you have any questions or concerns regarding the project success criteria review. I am always available to discuss this further and provide any additional support that you may need.

Thank you for your support and guidance on this project. I look forward to continuing to work together to ensure its success.

Best regards,
[Your Name]

EMAIL 73: ALIGNING VENDOR PRODUCT ROADMAPS FOR OPTIMAL SUCCESS

Aligning vendor product roadmaps is a crucial aspect of ensuring successful product development and delivery. By working together to ensure that product roadmaps align with company goals, software project managers can improve vendor relationships and product quality. This not only benefits the company and its customers but also strengthens the partnership between the company and the vendor. Effective alignment of vendor product roadmaps also helps ensure that resources are used efficiently and that project timelines are met. By prioritizing vendor alignment, software project managers can set their projects up for success and build strong relationships that benefit all parties involved.

Sample Email:

Subject Line: Product Roadmap Alignment Discussion for [Product Name]

Dear [Vendor Name],

I hope this email finds you well. I wanted to reach out to you regarding our [Product Name] roadmap and ensure that it aligns with our company goals. As you know, we highly value the products and services that your company provides, and we believe that by working together, we can create a highly successful partnership.

To that end, I would like to discuss with you any potential changes or updates that can be made to the [Product Name] roadmap to better align with our company goals. This will enable us to work together more effectively and efficiently, and improve both vendor relationships and product quality.

I understand that this may require some additional effort on your part, but I am confident that by working together, we can achieve great success and create a highly valuable product for our customers.

Please let me know if you have any questions or concerns regarding the alignment of the product roadmap or any other aspects of our partnership. I am more than happy to discuss this with you further and provide any additional support that you may need.

Thank you for your attention to this matter, and I look forward to continuing our successful partnership.

Best regards,
[Your Name]

EMAIL 74: BOOST YOUR SALES STRATEGY WITH CUSTOMER SEGMENTATION ANALYSIS

Customer segmentation analysis is a powerful tool that can help you identify potential opportunities and improve your sales strategy. By analyzing your customer base and identifying key segments, you can tailor your sales approach to the unique needs and preferences of each segment, resulting in increased sales and revenue.

With the right approach and the right tools, customer segmentation analysis can be a game-changer for your sales strategy. By focusing your efforts on the areas where you have the greatest potential for success, you can achieve greater results and take your sales performance to the next level.

Sample Email:

Subject Line: Customer Segmentation Analysis for [Product Name]

Dear [Sales Team],

I hope this email finds you well. As part of our ongoing efforts to improve our sales strategy for [Product Name], I wanted to share with you some findings from our recent customer segmentation analysis.

After analyzing our customer base, we have identified several key segments that we believe represent significant potential opportunities for increased product sales and revenue. Specifically, we have identified [segment 1, segment 2, etc.] as areas where we could make targeted efforts to improve our sales performance.

I would like to request your assistance in developing a targeted sales approach for each of these segments. By tailoring our sales efforts to the unique needs and preferences of each segment, we can better position ourselves for success and increase our overall sales performance.

I understand that this may require some additional effort on your part, but I strongly believe that it will be well worth it in the long run. By focusing our efforts on the areas where we have the greatest potential for success, we can improve our product sales and revenue and achieve greater success as a team.

Please let me know if you have any questions or concerns regarding this analysis or the proposed approach. I would be more than happy to discuss this with you further and provide any additional support that you may need.

Thank you for your hard work and dedication to our sales strategy for [Product Name]. I look forward to continuing to work with you to achieve our goals.

Best regards,

RAHUL PARMAR

[Your Name]

EMAIL 75: PRODUCT INTEGRATION PLAN FOR [PROJECT NAME]

Proper integration of various components is critical to the overall success of a project. Without a well-defined product integration plan in place, development teams may encounter issues that can lead to delays and setbacks during the development process. By developing a solid product integration plan, software project managers can greatly improve the overall quality of the product and increase customer satisfaction. This not only ensures that the product functions correctly but also provides a seamless experience for customers. A well-planned integration also minimizes the risk of errors and system crashes, allowing software developers to focus on developing and releasing new features, updates, and enhancements. In short, a product integration plan is a critical component of successful software development, and software project managers must ensure that it is properly planned and executed.

Sample Email:

Subject Line: Product Integration Plan for [Project Name]

Dear [Developer Name],

I hope this email finds you well. As we continue to work on [Project Name], I wanted to touch base with you regarding the product integration plan. As you are aware, proper integration of the various components is critical to the overall success of the project.

I would like to work with you to ensure that we have a well-defined plan for managing product integrations. This will involve a thorough analysis of the current product architecture and identifying any potential issues or roadblocks. We will also need to ensure that we have the necessary resources and expertise in place to address any challenges that may arise.

By having a solid product integration plan in place, we can greatly improve the overall quality of the product and increase customer satisfaction. This will also help us to minimize the risk of delays and setbacks during the development process.

I look forward to discussing this further with you and getting your input on the product integration plan. Please let me know if you have any questions or concerns, and we can set up a time to meet and discuss this in more detail.

Thank you for your hard work and dedication to this project. Your expertise and insights are greatly appreciated, and I am confident that we can work together to achieve success.

Best regards,
[Your Name]

EMAIL 76: PROJECT REQUIREMENTS VALIDATION

Validating project requirements with stakeholders has several benefits. Firstly, it helps to improve project success rates by ensuring that the project meets the needs of all stakeholders and is delivered on time and on budget. This, in turn, helps to build trust and credibility with stakeholders and can lead to future business opportunities.

Secondly, it improves stakeholder satisfaction by ensuring that their needs and expectations are understood and incorporated into the project. This can lead to increased engagement, buy-in, and support from stakeholders, which is critical to the success of any project.

Sample Email:

Subject Line: Project Requirements Validation for [Project Name]

Dear [Functional Manager Name],

I hope this email finds you well. I wanted to touch base with you regarding the project requirements for [Project Name]. As the software project manager, I am responsible for ensuring that the project requirements are fully validated with all stakeholders to ensure its success.

To that end, I wanted to schedule a meeting with you and other relevant stakeholders to go over the project requirements in detail. This will allow us to ensure that all requirements are clearly defined, understood, and agreed upon. It will also give us an opportunity to address any concerns or issues that may have arisen since the initial requirements gathering process.

By validating the project requirements with all stakeholders, we can ensure that the project is delivered on time, on budget, and meets the needs of all stakeholders. This will ultimately lead to improved project success rates and stakeholder satisfaction.

Please let me know if you have any questions or concerns, or if you have any preferred meeting times. I am looking forward to our discussion and working with you to ensure the success of [Project Name].

Best regards,
[Your Name]

EMAIL 77: PROJECT PERFORMANCE METRICS REVIEW

As a software project manager, reviewing project performance metrics is critical to the success of your projects. By identifying areas for improvement, you can ensure that your project stays on track, delivers high-quality results, and meets stakeholder expectations. Reviewing project performance metrics also allows you to make data-driven decisions and communicate progress effectively to your team and stakeholders. With the right approach and tools, you can streamline the process of reviewing project performance metrics and achieve greater project success rates and stakeholder satisfaction.

Sample Email:

Subject Line: Project Performance Metrics Review for [Project Name]

Dear [Boss's Name],

I hope this email finds you well. I wanted to take a moment to provide an update on the project performance metrics for [Project Name]. As the software project manager, I have been monitoring the metrics closely and have identified a few areas where we could make some improvements.

Specifically, I have noticed that the project timeline is slightly behind schedule, and the team has been experiencing some challenges with communication and collaboration. To address these issues, I have implemented a few changes in the project plan and have been working closely with the team to ensure that we are back on track.

In addition, I have also identified a few areas where we can improve the project's performance and efficiency. For example, by implementing a few process improvements and leveraging new technologies, we can improve the quality of our deliverables and streamline our development processes.

I strongly believe that by addressing these issues and implementing the necessary changes, we can improve the project's success rates and stakeholder satisfaction. I would be happy to provide a more detailed report on the project performance metrics and the changes that have been made upon your request.

Thank you for your attention to this matter, and please let me know if you have any questions or concerns.

Best regards,
[Your Name]

EMAIL 78: DISCUSSING PRODUCT TESTING PLAN WITH VENDORS

Effective communication and collaboration with vendors is essential to ensure high-quality products that meet the expectations of customers. By discussing the product testing plan with vendors, software project managers can ensure that testing criteria and methods are aligned, potential challenges are identified, and solutions are developed collaboratively. This helps to build stronger relationships with vendors and improves the quality of products, ultimately leading to increased customer satisfaction and loyalty. Additionally, effective collaboration with vendors can lead to cost savings and increased efficiency in the product development process. By prioritizing effective communication with vendors, software project managers can ensure the success of their projects and contribute to the overall success of their organizations.

Sample Email:

Subject Line: Product Testing Plan Discussion for [Product Name]

Dear [Vendor Name],

I hope this email finds you well. I wanted to touch base with you regarding the product testing plan for [Product Name]. As you know, this is a critical aspect of the product development process and it is important that we work together to ensure its success.

I would like to schedule a time to discuss the product testing plan in more detail and ensure that we are aligned on the approach. Specifically, I would like to review the testing criteria and methods that will be used to validate the product. Additionally, we can discuss any potential challenges or issues that may arise during the testing process and how we can work together to overcome them.

By having an open and collaborative discussion about the product testing plan, we can improve our vendor relationship and ensure that the product quality meets the highest standards. This will ultimately benefit both of our organizations and our customers.

Please let me know your availability over the next few days to schedule this discussion. I look forward to hearing from you and working together to ensure the success of [Product Name].

Best regards,
[Your Name]

EMAIL 79: PRODUCT SALES TRAINING PLAN FOR [PRODUCT NAME]

In today's fast-paced business environment, it is more important than ever to have a well-trained and equipped sales team. A product sales training plan can provide your team with the knowledge and skills they need to effectively promote and sell your product. By investing in sales training, you can increase your team's sales skills and expertise, which can translate into increased revenue and success for your company. A well-trained sales team can also lead to increased customer satisfaction and loyalty, as they are better equipped to understand and meet your customers' needs. So if you want to take your sales to the next level, consider developing a product sales training plan for your team today.

Sample Email:

Subject Line: Product Sales Training Plan for [Product Name]

Dear [Sales Team Name],

I hope this email finds you well. As you know, we will soon be launching [Product Name], and in order to maximize its success, it is essential that we have a well-trained and equipped sales team. Therefore, I am pleased to share with you the product sales training plan that I have developed for [Product Name].

The product sales training plan is designed to provide you with the necessary knowledge and skills to effectively promote and sell [Product Name]. The training will cover key features and benefits of the product, as well as the target audience and their pain points. Additionally, the training will include role-playing exercises and case studies to help you better understand how to sell the product in real-world situations.

I understand that your time is valuable, and I have therefore ensured that the training is as efficient and effective as possible. The training will be delivered via a combination of online modules and in-person sessions, with ample opportunities for Q&A and discussion.

I am confident that the product sales training plan will provide you with the tools and knowledge you need to effectively promote and sell [Product Name]. By increasing our sales skills and expertise, we can drive increased revenue and success for the company.

Please let me know if you have any questions or concerns regarding the product sales training plan. I would be more than happy to discuss this with you further and provide any additional support that you may need.

Thank you for your continued dedication and hard work. I look forward to seeing the positive impact of the product sales training plan on our sales and revenue.

RAHUL PARMAR

Best regards,
[Your Name]

EMAIL 80: PRIORITIZING PRODUCT FEATURES FOR SUCCESSFUL SOFTWARE PROJECTS

Prioritizing product features is a critical step in ensuring the success of any software project. By identifying and focusing on the most important features, software project managers can improve product quality and customer satisfaction, while also maximizing development efficiency and ensuring on-time delivery. By working with developers and other stakeholders to create a feature prioritization plan, software project managers can ensure that their projects are aligned with business goals and customer needs. With the right prioritization strategy in place, software project managers can achieve project success and drive business growth.

Sample Email:

Subject Line: Product Feature Prioritization for [Project Name]

Dear [Developer Name],

I hope you are doing well. I wanted to reach out to you today regarding the product feature prioritization for [Project Name]. As you know, one of the key challenges of any software project is deciding which features should be prioritized and which ones should be delayed or cut.

I believe that we can greatly improve the product quality and customer satisfaction by making sure that we prioritize the right features. To that end, I would like to work with you and the rest of the development team to create a feature prioritization plan for the project.

To get started, I would like to request your input on the features that you think should be prioritized. We will also need to consider factors such as the project timeline, budget, and customer feedback. Once we have identified the top priority features, we can start working on them immediately and ensure that they are completed to the highest standards.

I understand that this may require some additional effort on your part, but I believe that the benefits will be well worth it. By prioritizing the right features, we can ensure that the product meets the needs of our customers and stands out in the marketplace.

Please let me know if you have any questions or concerns regarding this project. I am excited to work with you on this and look forward to hearing your input.

Best regards,
[Your Name]

EMAIL 81: IMPROVING STAKEHOLDER ENGAGEMENT IN SOFTWARE PROJECTS

Proactively engaging with project stakeholders is essential for the success of software projects. By gathering feedback and addressing concerns, software project managers can ensure that stakeholders feel heard and valued, leading to improved project success rates and stakeholder satisfaction. A stakeholder engagement plan can help project managers proactively engage with stakeholders by outlining various activities, such as regular check-ins, status updates, and surveys, to gather feedback and address concerns. By implementing a stakeholder engagement plan, software project managers can increase the likelihood of project success and improve stakeholder satisfaction, leading to long-term benefits for the organization.

Sample Email:

Subject Line: Project Stakeholder Engagement Plan for [Project Name]

Dear [Functional Manager Name],

I hope this email finds you well. I am writing to discuss the stakeholder engagement plan for our project, [Project Name]. As you know, stakeholder engagement is critical to the success of any project, and I believe we can make some improvements in this area.

To that end, I have developed a stakeholder engagement plan that outlines the various activities that we will undertake to engage with our stakeholders. The plan includes regular check-ins with stakeholders, status updates, and stakeholder surveys to gather feedback on the project's progress.

I believe that by proactively engaging with our stakeholders, we can improve the project's success rates and increase stakeholder satisfaction. By gathering feedback and addressing concerns, we can ensure that our stakeholders feel heard and valued, which will ultimately lead to better project outcomes.

I would like to schedule a meeting with you to discuss this plan in further detail and get your feedback. I am open to any suggestions or ideas that you may have, and I welcome your input in this process.

Thank you for your attention to this matter. I look forward to working with you to ensure the success of this project.

Best regards,
[Your Name]

EMAIL 82: PROJECT PHASE GATE REVIEW

As a software project manager, reviewing project phase gates is a critical component of project success. It ensures that the project is on track to meet its objectives and stakeholder requirements, while also identifying potential issues and making necessary adjustments. A project phase gate review meeting with your boss provides an opportunity to align with project goals, discuss progress, and identify any potential roadblocks. By doing so, you can ensure that the project is delivered on time and to the highest quality standards, which will increase project success rates and stakeholder satisfaction. A well-executed project phase gate review can also help to keep the team aligned and motivated towards a common goal. So, be sure to schedule regular project phase gate review meetings and use them to your advantage.

Sample Email:

Subject Line: Project Phase Gate Review for [Project Name]

Dear [Boss Name],

I hope this email finds you well. I wanted to provide you with an update on our progress with the [Project Name] project. As we approach the next phase gate, I wanted to take a moment to review our progress and ensure alignment with our project goals.

During the previous phase, we faced a few challenges, but the team was able to work together to overcome them successfully. Moving forward, I believe we are on track to meet our objectives for this phase and deliver the project on time and to the highest quality standards.

To ensure we are aligned with our project goals and meet stakeholder satisfaction, I would like to schedule a project phase gate review meeting with you. During the meeting, we will discuss our progress, review the project goals, and ensure we are meeting stakeholder requirements.

I am confident that this meeting will help us to identify any potential issues and make any necessary adjustments to ensure the success of the project. It will also provide an opportunity to celebrate the accomplishments of the team and keep everyone aligned and motivated.

Please let me know if there are any specific items that you would like to cover during the review meeting, and I will be sure to include them on the agenda.

Thank you for your continued support of this project, and I look forward to speaking with you soon.

Best regards,
[Your Name]

EMAIL 83: IMPROVE VENDOR RELATIONSHIPS AND PRODUCT QUALITY

Effective communication with vendors is key to ensuring successful product development and delivery. By conducting a product feature gap analysis and sharing the findings with your vendors, you not only demonstrate your commitment to improving the product but also strengthen your partnership and collaboration. By working together to address these gaps, you can ensure that the product meets the needs of your customers and is of the highest quality. This not only improves the product's value proposition but also increases customer satisfaction and loyalty. So, take the time to communicate with your vendors and work together to improve the product. The results will be worth it!

Sample Email:

Subject Line: Product Feature Gap Analysis for [Product Name]

Dear [Vendor Name],

I hope this email finds you well. I wanted to take a moment to discuss the product feature gap analysis for [Product Name] and share our findings with you.

Firstly, I wanted to thank you for your partnership and collaboration on this project. We greatly value our relationship with you and appreciate your hard work and dedication to delivering a quality product.

As part of our ongoing efforts to improve the product, we conducted a feature gap analysis to identify areas where we could enhance the product and better meet our customers' needs. During this analysis, we identified a few areas where we believe there are opportunities to improve the product and close feature gaps.

I would like to discuss these findings with you and explore potential solutions to address these gaps. I believe that by working together, we can strengthen our partnership and deliver an even better product to our customers.

Please let me know if you are available to schedule a call or meeting to discuss this further. I look forward to hearing from you soon and continuing to work together to improve [Product Name].

Thank you again for your hard work and partnership.

Best regards,
[Your Name]

EMAIL 84: DEVELOPING EFFECTIVE PRODUCT VALUE PROPOSITION MESSAGING

Effective product value proposition messaging is essential for any business looking to succeed in the market. By clearly communicating the unique value that your product provides to customers, you can differentiate yourself from competitors and attract potential customers to your brand. With the right messaging, you can increase your product sales and revenue, build customer loyalty, and ultimately, achieve long-term success.

But developing effective messaging can be a challenge, especially if you're unsure of where to start. That's where our sample email comes in. By providing guidance on how to develop effective product value proposition messaging, we can help you create messaging that resonates with your customers and drives sales.

Sample Email:

Subject Line: Product Value Proposition Messaging for [Product Name]

Dear [Sales Team],

I hope this email finds you well. As we prepare to launch [Product Name], I wanted to provide you with some guidance on the product's value proposition messaging. As you know, effective messaging is critical to the success of our product and can greatly impact our sales and revenue.

In developing our value proposition messaging, we need to focus on the key benefits that [Product Name] provides to our customers. These benefits should be centered around solving our customers' pain points and addressing their needs. Our messaging should clearly communicate how our product stands out from our competitors and how it provides unique value to our customers.

To develop effective messaging, I recommend that you use customer feedback and testimonials. This will help us to better understand our customers' needs and the benefits that they value the most. Additionally, we should focus on using simple and concise language to convey our message effectively.

I understand that developing messaging can be challenging, but it is an essential part of our sales strategy. By creating effective messaging, we can increase our product sales and revenue, and ultimately, our success in the market.

Please let me know if you have any questions or if you need any additional support. I am here to help and look forward to working with you to ensure the success of [Product Name].

Best regards,
[Your Name]

EMAIL 85: IMPROVING PRODUCT PERFORMANCE THROUGH BENCHMARKING

Benchmarking product performance is an essential component of delivering high-quality products and achieving customer satisfaction. By identifying areas for improvement, software project managers can optimize product speed and responsiveness while reducing the overall memory footprint. This not only improves the overall product quality but also increases customer loyalty and drives sales and revenue. By scheduling a meeting with the development team to discuss specific areas for improvement, project managers can ensure that their products are meeting the highest standards and providing customers with the best possible experience.

Sample Email:

Subject Line: Product Performance Benchmarking for [Project Name]

Dear [Developer Name],

I hope this email finds you well. I wanted to take a moment to discuss the product performance benchmarking for [Project Name]. As you know, we are committed to delivering the highest quality products to our customers, and benchmarking product performance is an essential part of this process.

I have been reviewing the recent performance benchmarks and noticed a few areas where we could make some improvements. Specifically, we need to focus on optimizing the product's speed and responsiveness, as well as reducing the overall memory footprint.

By improving the product's performance, we can ensure that our customers have a seamless and efficient experience while using our product. This, in turn, will increase customer satisfaction and loyalty, ultimately driving sales and revenue.

I would like to schedule a meeting with you and the team to discuss these findings further and identify specific areas for improvement. Please let me know your availability so that we can schedule a time that works for everyone.

Thank you for your hard work and dedication to this project. I look forward to working with you to improve the product's performance and quality.

Best regards,
[Your Name]

EMAIL 86: IMPROVE YOUR PROJECT SUCCESS RATES WITH EFFECTIVE CHANGE MANAGEMENT

Change is inevitable in any project, but it can also be a major source of risk and uncertainty. Without a proper plan in place, changes can lead to delays, cost overruns, and stakeholder dissatisfaction. That's why effective change management is crucial for project success. By implementing a change management process that includes a thorough review of all change requests, a risk assessment, and a clear protocol for handling any potential issues, you can ensure that your project stays on track and is completed to the highest standards. With the right change management plan in place, you can greatly improve your project success rates and stakeholder satisfaction, and ensure that any changes to the project are managed effectively.

Sample Email:

Subject Line: Project Change Management Plan for [Project Name]

Dear [Functional Manager Name],

I hope this email finds you well. As we move forward with [Project Name], I wanted to take a moment to discuss our change management plan. As you know, change is an inevitable part of any project, and it is important that we have a plan in place to manage it effectively.

I propose that we implement a change management process that includes a thorough review of all change requests, a risk assessment, and a plan for communicating any changes to relevant stakeholders. By doing so, we can ensure that all changes are properly evaluated, and their impact on the project is fully understood.

In addition to this, I suggest that we develop a clear protocol for handling any potential issues or challenges that arise as a result of changes to the project. This will allow us to quickly identify and address any issues before they can escalate, ensuring that the project stays on track and is completed to the highest standards.

By planning and executing a change management plan for [Project Name], we can greatly improve our project success rates and stakeholder satisfaction. We can also ensure that any changes to the project are managed effectively, and that their impact on the project is fully understood.

Please let me know your thoughts on this proposal, and if you have any suggestions or concerns. I look forward to working with you to ensure the success of [Project Name].

Best regards,
[Your Name]

EMAIL 87: PROVIDING PROJECT STATUS REPORTS TO BOSSES

Regular project status reports provide several key benefits to software project managers and their stakeholders. Firstly, they help to improve communication and visibility, ensuring that all stakeholders are on the same page regarding project progress. Secondly, they provide an opportunity for early identification of potential issues or challenges, allowing for timely intervention and mitigation. Finally, they enable project managers to build trust and credibility with their stakeholders, demonstrating a commitment to transparency and accountability.

Sample Email:

Subject Line: Project Status Report for [Project Name]

Dear [Boss's Name],

I hope this email finds you well. I wanted to provide you with a project status report for [Project Name] to ensure that you are up-to-date on its progress. As you know, regular project status reports are an important part of effective project management, and I want to make sure that we are all on the same page regarding the project's status.

Overall, I am pleased to report that the project is progressing well and is on track to meet its timeline and budget goals. The team has been working hard to complete the project tasks and deliverables according to the project plan, and we have made some excellent progress in the past few weeks.

There are a few areas where we have encountered some challenges, however. Specifically, we have experienced some delays in acquiring the necessary resources for a critical task, which has caused a delay in the overall project timeline. We are actively working to address this issue and are exploring all available options to mitigate the impact on the project's timeline and budget.

Moving forward, we will continue to closely monitor the project's progress and provide regular updates to all stakeholders. If you have any questions or concerns regarding the project status or the challenges we are facing, please don't hesitate to reach out to me. I would be more than happy to discuss this with you further and provide any additional information or support that you may need.

Thank you for your ongoing support and guidance throughout this project. We greatly appreciate your leadership and look forward to successfully completing this project together.

Best regards,
[Your Name]

EMAIL 88: NEED TO UPDATE VENDOR PRODUCT ROADMAPS TO ALIGN WITH COMPANY GOALS

Effective communication with vendors is critical to the success of any software project. By providing regular updates on product roadmaps and ensuring alignment with company goals, software project managers can improve vendor relationships and product quality. This not only helps to ensure the success of the project but also lays the foundation for future collaborations and partnerships. The email template provided above is an example of how software project managers can communicate effectively with vendors to ensure that the project stays on track and meets its goals. By using this template and others like it from "The Ultimate Resource for Software Project Managers: 100 Email Templates for Every Project Scenario," software project managers can improve their communication skills and achieve success in their projects.

Sample Email:

Subject Line: Product Roadmap Alignment Update for [Product Name]

Dear [Vendor Name],

I hope this email finds you well. I wanted to take a moment to update you on our product roadmap for [Product Name]. As you know, we have been working hard to align our company goals with the development of this product, and I wanted to ensure that our roadmap is in line with our shared vision.

To that end, I have reviewed our current roadmap and identified a few areas where we could make some improvements. Specifically, I think we should focus on [specific areas where changes are needed]. I would greatly appreciate your feedback on these proposed changes, as well as any other suggestions you may have.

I understand that these changes may require some adjustments on your part, and I want to assure you that we value your partnership and the contributions you have made to this project so far. By aligning our product roadmap with our company goals, we can improve our vendor relationships and product quality, and ensure the success of this project.

Please let me know if you have any questions or concerns regarding the proposed changes. I look forward to continuing to work with you to ensure the success of [Product Name].

Thank you again for your hard work and dedication to this project.

Best regards,
[Your Name]

EMAIL 89: PROVIDING PRODUCT OBJECTION HANDLING TRAINING FOR SALES TEAM

Effective objection handling is critical to achieving success in sales, and providing training for the sales team can have a significant impact on increasing product sales and revenue. By addressing common objections and providing effective solutions, sales team members can feel more confident and prepared when speaking with customers, leading to increased customer satisfaction and improved sales performance. Additionally, providing product objection handling training can improve the overall reputation of the company, as customers are more likely to recommend a product or service to others if they feel their concerns have been addressed effectively. Investing in product objection handling training is an investment in the long-term success of the company, and can lead to improved sales performance and increased revenue over time.

Sample Email:

Subject Line: Product Objection Handling Training for [Product Name]

Dear [Sales Team],

I hope this email finds you well. As we continue to work towards increasing product sales and revenue, it has become clear that we need to provide some additional support to the sales team in terms of product objection handling.

Therefore, I am excited to announce that we will be providing product objection handling training for [Product Name] in the coming weeks. This training will be designed to provide you with the knowledge and skills necessary to address common objections that customers may have, and help you to close more sales as a result.

The training will cover a range of topics, including identifying common objections, understanding the underlying concerns, and providing effective solutions to address them. We will also be providing you with some practical tools and techniques to use in real-world scenarios, to help you feel confident and prepared when speaking with customers.

I strongly encourage all members of the sales team to attend this training, as it will be an invaluable resource in helping us to achieve our goals. By improving our objection handling skills, we can ensure that we are effectively communicating the value of [Product Name], and addressing any concerns that customers may have.

Please let me know if you have any questions or concerns regarding the training. I would be more than happy to discuss this with you further and provide any additional support that you may need.

Thank you for your continued hard work and dedication to the success of [Product Name]. I look forward to working with you to achieve our goals.

Best regards,
[Your Name]

EMAIL 90: ALIGNING PRODUCT ROADMAP WITH COMPANY GOALS

Aligning your product roadmap with your company's goals is crucial for the success of your business. By doing so, you ensure that your products are meeting the needs and expectations of your customers, which ultimately leads to improved product quality and customer satisfaction. This not only benefits your customers but also your business in the long run. With a well-aligned product roadmap, you can improve the overall success of your projects and ensure that you are delivering value to your customers. So take the time to analyze your company's goals and align your product roadmap accordingly. Your customers and your business will thank you for it.

Sample Email:

Subject Line: Product Roadmap Alignment Plan for [Project Name]

Dear [Developer Name],

I hope this email finds you well. As we continue to work on [Project Name], I wanted to take a moment to discuss the importance of aligning the project roadmap with the company's goals.

By aligning the project roadmap with company goals, we can ensure that the product we are developing meets the needs and expectations of our customers. This not only improves the product quality but also enhances customer satisfaction, which is essential for the long-term success of our business.

To achieve this, I would like to propose a product roadmap alignment plan. This plan will involve a thorough analysis of the company's goals, as well as a review of the current project roadmap. From there, we can identify any areas where adjustments need to be made to better align the project roadmap with company goals.

I understand that this may require some additional work on your part, but I am confident that the end result will be worth it. By ensuring that the project is aligned with the company's goals, we can improve the overall success of the project and the business as a whole.

Please let me know if you have any questions or concerns regarding this plan. I would be more than happy to discuss this with you further and provide any additional support that you may need.

Thank you for your hard work and dedication to this project. I look forward to continuing to work with you to ensure its success.

Best regards,
[Your Name]

EMAIL 91: EFFECTIVE PROJECT RESOURCE ALLOCATION

Proper allocation of project resources is a crucial aspect of successful project management. By allocating resources efficiently, you can ensure that the project is completed within the designated timeline and budget. Additionally, proper resource allocation can help reduce unnecessary waste and increase productivity. It is essential to identify and allocate the necessary personnel, equipment, and tools required to complete the project successfully. A well-planned resource allocation plan will also help mitigate any risks or obstacles that may arise during the project's execution. By taking the time to plan and allocate resources effectively, you can improve project timelines and success rates, deliver a quality product to stakeholders, and ultimately achieve your project goals and objectives.

Sample Email:

Subject Line: Project Resource Allocation Plan for [Project Name]

Dear [Functional Manager Name],

I hope this email finds you well. As we continue to move forward with [Project Name], I wanted to touch base with you regarding the project's resource allocation plan. I believe it is essential to ensure that the project has the necessary resources allocated effectively to guarantee its success.

Based on our previous discussions and the project requirements, I have developed a preliminary resource allocation plan. This plan outlines the necessary personnel, equipment, and tools required to complete the project successfully. It also provides timelines and costs associated with each resource allocation.

I would appreciate it if you could take some time to review the plan and provide any feedback or recommendations you may have. I believe that your insight and expertise will be crucial in ensuring that the plan is comprehensive and effective.

By allocating resources efficiently, we can improve project timelines and success rates. This, in turn, will help us to achieve our project goals and objectives while delivering a quality product to our stakeholders.

Thank you in advance for your attention to this matter. Please let me know if you have any questions or concerns regarding the resource allocation plan.

Best regards,
[Your Name]

EMAIL 92: PROJECT BUDGET REVIEW

As a software project manager, reviewing the project budget regularly is crucial for successful project delivery. It ensures that the project is on track to meet financial goals and helps to avoid any unforeseen financial risks. By reallocating funds and reducing costs in certain areas, the project can be completed on time and within budget. Regular budget reviews also provide greater transparency and improve financial planning. This email template provides a clear and concise way to communicate budget updates to your boss, ensuring that everyone is on the same page and working towards the same financial goals.

Sample Email:

Subject Line: Project Budget Review for [Project Name]

Dear [Boss's Name],

I hope this email finds you well. I wanted to provide an update on the budget for [Project Name]. As we are nearing the end of the quarter, I wanted to ensure that we are on track to meet our financial goals and that there are no surprises in the coming weeks.

After reviewing the budget for [Project Name], I have identified a few areas where we can make some adjustments. Specifically, I believe that we can reallocate some of the funds to ensure that we are investing in the areas that will provide the most value for the project. Additionally, there may be some opportunities to reduce costs in certain areas without compromising the project's success.

I believe that by reviewing the budget regularly, we can ensure that we are making the best use of our resources and that we are able to deliver the project on time and within budget. This will also provide greater transparency and help to avoid any unforeseen financial risks.

Please let me know if you have any questions or concerns regarding the budget review. I am happy to provide any additional information or support that you may need.

Thank you for your continued support and leadership on this project.

Best regards,
[Your Name]

EMAIL 93: PRODUCT PRICING NEGOTIATION WITH VENDORS

Effective pricing negotiations can lead to improved vendor relationships and streamlined procurement processes. By initiating pricing negotiations, you can demonstrate to vendors that you value their partnership while also ensuring that you are receiving competitive pricing for the product. This can lead to long-term vendor relationships built on trust and mutual benefit. Additionally, efficient procurement processes can save your company time and resources while ensuring the continued success of your projects.

Sample Email:

Subject Line: Product Pricing Negotiation for [Product Name]

Dear [Vendor Name],

I hope this email finds you well. As we move forward with [Product Name], I wanted to touch base with you regarding the pricing for the product. While we greatly value the partnership we have with your company, we also need to ensure that we are receiving competitive pricing for the product.

With that in mind, I would like to initiate a pricing negotiation for [Product Name]. I believe that there is an opportunity for us to work together to find a mutually beneficial pricing structure that aligns with our budget and procurement processes, while also maintaining a positive vendor relationship.

In order to achieve this, I would like to schedule a call to discuss the pricing structure and explore any potential options for cost savings. I am confident that we can find a solution that works for both parties and ensures the continued success of our partnership.

Please let me know your availability in the coming week to schedule a call. I look forward to discussing this further with you.

Thank you for your time and attention to this matter.

Best regards,
[Your Name]

EMAIL 94: DEVELOPING CUSTOMER SUCCESS STORIES FOR INCREASED SALES

Customer success stories are a powerful tool for increasing product sales and revenue. By showcasing the positive experiences of satisfied customers, potential customers can see the value and potential of the product. This can build trust and credibility, and ultimately lead to increased sales. Developing customer success stories can also help to differentiate the product from competitors and position it as a valuable solution for customers' needs. Overall, investing time and resources into developing customer success stories is a smart strategy for any company looking to increase sales and grow its customer base.

Sample Email:

Subject Line: Customer Success Story Development for [Product Name]

Dear [Sales Team],

I hope this email finds you well. As we continue to promote [Product Name] to potential customers, I wanted to emphasize the importance of customer success stories in our marketing efforts. By showcasing the successes that our customers have achieved with our product, we can demonstrate its value and build trust with new prospects.

To that end, I would like to request your assistance in identifying and developing customer success stories for [Product Name]. I would like to feature these stories on our website, in our marketing materials, and in our sales presentations to help promote the product.

I believe that by sharing the experiences of our satisfied customers, we can increase our product sales and revenue, and build a strong reputation for [Product Name] in the market.

Please let me know if you have any questions or concerns regarding this request. I would be more than happy to discuss this with you further and provide any additional support that you may need.

Thank you for your hard work and dedication to promoting [Product Name]. I look forward to working with you to develop these customer success stories and continue to grow our customer base.

Best regards,
[Your Name]

EMAIL 95: PROVIDING FEEDBACK ON PROJECT CODE REVIEWS

By providing feedback on project code reviews, you can identify potential issues and areas for improvement, which can help improve the code quality and development efficiency. This can ultimately lead to fewer errors and bugs in the future, as well as a more streamlined development process. Additionally, providing feedback can also help your team members grow and improve their skills, which can benefit the project as a whole. By taking the time to provide feedback on project code reviews, you can help ensure the success of your projects and the continued growth of your team members.

Sample Email:

Subject Line: Project Code Review Feedback for [Project Name]

Dear [Developer Name],

I hope this email finds you well. I wanted to take a moment to provide feedback on the code review for [Project Name]. Firstly, I wanted to thank you and the team for your hard work and dedication to the project.

During the code review, I noticed several areas where we can make some improvements to the codebase. Specifically, I would like to suggest a few changes to improve the code quality and development efficiency. There were some instances where we can make the code more modular and easier to maintain, which will save us time and effort in the long run.

I understand that these changes may require additional time and effort on your part, but I believe that they are necessary to ensure that the project is completed on time and to the highest quality standards. By improving the code quality and development efficiency, we can also reduce the likelihood of errors and bugs in the future.

Please let me know if you have any questions or concerns regarding the feedback provided. I am available to discuss this further and provide any additional support you may need.

Thank you again for your hard work and dedication to the project. I look forward to working with you to ensure its continued success.

Best regards,
[Your Name]

EMAIL 96: REGULAR PROJECT PROGRESS UPDATES FOR FUNCTIONAL MANAGERS

Regular project progress updates for functional managers improve communication and visibility for stakeholders, allowing them to have a better understanding of the project's progress and any challenges that have arisen. This increased visibility ensures that stakeholders are able to make informed decisions, offer support, and provide feedback. By providing these updates, software project managers can increase stakeholder engagement and satisfaction, leading to a higher likelihood of project success. Additionally, regular updates can help to prevent miscommunication or misunderstandings, which can lead to delays or other issues in the project.

Sample Email:

Subject Line: Project Progress Update for [Project Name]

Dear [Functional Manager Name],

I hope this email finds you well. I wanted to provide you with an update on the progress of [Project Name]. As you know, this project is a top priority for our company, and I wanted to ensure that you are aware of the progress that has been made so far.

To date, we have completed [list key achievements or milestones reached]. Additionally, we are currently on schedule to complete the project on time and within budget. However, we have encountered a few challenges along the way, including [list any issues or concerns that have arisen].

I want to assure you that we are taking steps to address these challenges and ensure that the project remains on track. Specifically, we are [list any actions being taken to address the challenges]. We are also continuously reviewing our processes and making improvements to ensure that we are delivering the highest quality work possible.

I believe that by providing regular project progress updates, we can ensure that you and other stakeholders have visibility into the project and can make any necessary adjustments or provide support as needed. If you have any questions or concerns regarding the project or its progress, please don't hesitate to reach out to me.

Thank you for your continued support and engagement with this project. I look forward to providing you with further updates as the project progresses.

Best regards,
[Your Name]

EMAIL 97: PROJECT RESOURCE FORECASTING

Proper project resource forecasting provides numerous benefits, including improved project success rates and timelines. By accurately forecasting resource needs, managers can ensure that they have the necessary staff, equipment, and materials to complete the project on time and within budget. This leads to higher quality products, increased customer satisfaction, and a stronger reputation for the company. Additionally, effective forecasting can help managers identify potential risks or obstacles and develop strategies to mitigate them, further increasing the chances of project success. Overall, investing time and effort into project resource forecasting is crucial for any software project manager looking to achieve success.

Sample Email:

Subject Line: Project Resource Forecasting for [Project Name]

Dear [Boss Name],

I hope this email finds you well. I wanted to provide an update on the project resource forecasting for [Project Name]. As you know, accurate forecasting is crucial for ensuring that we have the necessary resources to complete the project on time and within budget.

Based on our current projections, we will need to allocate additional resources to the project in order to meet our targets. Specifically, I believe that we will need to increase the number of developers working on the project in the coming weeks.

To ensure that we are able to secure the necessary resources, I have reached out to our HR department to discuss our options for hiring additional staff. I am also exploring the possibility of reallocating resources from other projects within the company, although I understand that this may not be feasible.

I wanted to bring this to your attention early in the process so that we can plan accordingly and avoid any delays or setbacks. By ensuring that we have the necessary resources, we can improve project timelines and success rates, and ultimately deliver a high-quality product to our customers.

Please let me know if you have any questions or concerns regarding the project resource forecasting. I would be happy to provide any additional information or support that you may need.

Thank you for your continued support of this project.

Best regards,
[Your Name]

EMAIL 98: PROVIDING VALUABLE FEEDBACK TO VENDORS

When you provide feedback to vendors on their product roadmaps, you show that you are invested in their success and that you care about the quality of the products they provide. This, in turn, can help to strengthen your vendor relationships and increase the likelihood of successful collaboration in the future. Additionally, by providing feedback on their product roadmaps, you can help vendors to improve the quality of their products, leading to increased customer satisfaction and improved market success. Overall, providing feedback to vendors is an essential component of successful software project management and can lead to significant benefits for both parties involved.

Sample Email:

Subject Line: Product Roadmap Feedback for [Product Name]

Dear [Vendor Name],

I hope this email finds you well. I wanted to take a moment to thank you and your team for the excellent work that has been done so far on [Product Name]. We greatly appreciate your dedication and hard work in bringing this product to market.

During our recent review of the product roadmap, I noticed a few areas where we could provide some feedback to help improve the product's development and market success. Specifically, I think we could benefit from additional focus on certain features that our customers have been requesting, and a more streamlined timeline to ensure that we meet their needs in a timely manner.

I understand that the product roadmap is a complex and ever-evolving process, and that these changes may require some additional effort on your part. However, I strongly believe that this feedback will greatly benefit both our organizations and ultimately lead to improved product quality and increased customer satisfaction.

I would be more than happy to discuss these changes with you in more detail and answer any questions you may have. Additionally, I would appreciate any feedback or suggestions that you may have in return.

Thank you again for your hard work and dedication to this project. I look forward to continuing to work with you to bring [Product Name] to market.

Best regards,
[Your Name]

EMAIL 99: SUCCESSFUL PRODUCT LAUNCH IS CRITICAL

A well-executed product launch can make or break the success of a product. It can generate excitement and interest in the product, resulting in increased sales and revenue. A product launch plan is a critical tool in ensuring a successful launch. It outlines all the necessary activities and tasks that need to be completed leading up to the launch date, ensuring that everything is completed on time and to the highest standards. By following a well-planned launch plan, you can maximize the potential of your product and achieve your sales goals. So, take the time to develop a comprehensive product launch plan and ensure the success of your product launch.

Sample Email:

Subject Line: Product Launch Plan for [Product Name]

Dear [Sales Team],

I hope this email finds you well. As you know, we are getting closer to the launch date for our new product, [Product Name]. In order to ensure a successful launch, I wanted to share with you the product launch plan that we have developed.

The product launch plan is a comprehensive guide that outlines all the activities and tasks that need to be completed leading up to the launch date. It covers everything from product messaging and positioning to promotional activities and launch events.

The success of our product launch is critical to achieving our sales goals and increasing revenue. A well-planned and executed launch can generate excitement and interest in the product, resulting in increased product sales and revenue.

I encourage you to review the product launch plan carefully and familiarize yourself with the activities and tasks that are outlined. It is important that we work together to ensure that everything is completed on time and to the highest standards.

Please let me know if you have any questions or concerns regarding the product launch plan. I would be more than happy to discuss this with you further and provide any additional support that you may need.

Thank you for your hard work and dedication to this project. I look forward to continuing to work with you to ensure its success.

Best regards,
[Your Name]

EMAIL 100: PRODUCT SECURITY ASSESSMENT

A product security assessment provides valuable insights into potential security risks and vulnerabilities, which can be addressed to improve the overall quality of the product. By identifying and addressing potential security risks early on, you can ensure that your product meets the highest security standards, providing your customers with peace of mind and improving their satisfaction with your product.

In addition to the direct benefits of improved product quality and customer satisfaction, conducting a product security assessment can also help you maintain your reputation as a company that takes security seriously. This can have a positive impact on your brand image and help you attract and retain customers.

Sample Email:

Subject Line: Product Security Assessment for [Project Name]

Dear [Developer Name],

I hope this email finds you well. I wanted to take a moment to discuss the importance of product security assessment for [Project Name]. As you know, security is an essential aspect of our product development process, and it is critical that we identify potential vulnerabilities early on in the project.

I would like to request that you and the team conduct a thorough product security assessment for [Project Name]. This will involve reviewing the code and infrastructure for potential security risks and identifying any areas where we can improve security.

By conducting this assessment, we can ensure that the product is developed to the highest security standards, which will improve the overall product quality and customer satisfaction. It will also ensure that we maintain our reputation as a company that takes security seriously.

I understand that conducting a security assessment can be a time-consuming process, but it is a necessary step in the development process. Please let me know if you have any questions or concerns regarding this request. I am happy to discuss this with you further and provide any additional support that you may need.

Thank you for your dedication and hard work on this project. I look forward to working with you to ensure its success.

Best regards,
[Your Name]

EMAIL 101: CLEAR AND EFFECTIVE ISSUE ESCALATION FOR IMPROVED PROJECT SUCCESS

As a software project manager, having a clear and effective issue escalation plan in place is critical to ensuring project success rates and stakeholder satisfaction. By creating and communicating a plan for issue escalation, project managers can minimize the impact of issues on the project and ensure that they are addressed in a timely and efficient manner. This not only leads to improved project success rates but also helps to build trust and confidence among stakeholders. With a well-defined issue escalation plan, software project managers can ensure that their projects stay on track and meet the needs of all stakeholders involved.

Sample Email:

Subject Line: Project Issue Escalation Plan for [Project Name]

Dear [Functional Manager Name],

I hope this email finds you well. As we move forward with [Project Name], I wanted to take a moment to discuss the importance of having a clear plan for issue escalation.

As you know, issues can arise at any point during a project, and it's critical that we have a plan in place to address them as quickly and effectively as possible. That's why I'm reaching out to you today to create and communicate a project issue escalation plan.

Having a clear and well-communicated plan in place for issue escalation will not only ensure that we can respond to issues in a timely manner but will also improve our project success rates and stakeholder satisfaction. By addressing issues quickly and effectively, we can minimize the impact they have on the project and ensure that we meet our goals and objectives.

To create this plan, I propose that we work together to define the key issue types that could arise during the project, determine the severity of each issue, and outline a clear escalation process for each type of issue. We can also identify the key stakeholders who should be involved in each escalation process.

I would be more than happy to set up a meeting to discuss this plan further and work with you to ensure that it meets the needs of the project and all stakeholders involved. Please let me know if you have any questions or concerns, and I look forward to hearing back from you soon.

Best regards,
[Your Name]

EMAIL 102: PROJECT CHANGE REQUEST STATUS UPDATE

As a software project manager, providing regular status updates on project change requests is crucial to ensuring project success rates and stakeholder satisfaction. By keeping your boss informed of the status of change requests, you can demonstrate your commitment to the project and your ability to manage change effectively. Regular updates can also help to identify potential risks and issues early on, allowing you to take corrective action and prevent them from becoming larger problems. Ultimately, providing status updates on change requests can help to ensure that the project is completed on time, within budget, and to the satisfaction of all stakeholders.

Sample Email:

Subject Line: Project Change Request Status Update for [Project Name]

Dear [Boss Name],

I hope this email finds you well. I wanted to provide you with a status update on the project change requests for [Project Name]. As you know, these change requests are crucial to the success of the project and require careful consideration and management.

Currently, we have received [number of change requests] change requests, all of which have been reviewed and assessed for their impact on the project. Of these requests, [number of approved requests] have been approved and are currently being incorporated into the project plan. The remaining requests are either under review or have been rejected due to their potential impact on the project timeline and budget.

I want to assure you that we are doing everything we can to ensure that the project stays on track while accommodating these change requests. Our team is working diligently to assess each request and its potential impact on the project, and we are committed to keeping you informed throughout the process.

I believe that by providing you with regular status updates on these change requests, we can ensure improved project success rates and stakeholder satisfaction. It is our goal to ensure that the project meets all expectations and is completed on time and within budget.

If you have any questions or concerns regarding the project change request status, please do not hesitate to reach out. We are always available to discuss this further and provide any additional information that you may need.

Thank you for your continued support and guidance throughout this project. We look forward to continuing to work with you to achieve its success.

Best regards,
[Your Name]

EMAIL 103: COMMUNICATING PRODUCT CERTIFICATION REQUIREMENTS TO VENDORS

By effectively communicating product certification requirements to vendors, software project managers can improve vendor relationships and streamline the procurement process. This can lead to improved collaboration and increased efficiency in the project delivery process. By clearly outlining the necessary certifications and timelines for completion, vendors can ensure that the procurement process is as smooth as possible, ultimately leading to successful project delivery. Effective communication with vendors can also help to establish trust and credibility, leading to stronger and more productive partnerships in the future. Overall, clear and effective communication around product certification requirements is essential for the success of software projects and the achievement of project goals.

Sample Email:

Subject Line: Product Certification Requirements for [Product Name]

Dear [Vendor Name],

I hope this email finds you well. I am writing to provide you with the product certification requirements for [Product Name] and to ensure that we are aligned on the necessary steps for certification.

As you know, certification is a critical part of the procurement process, and we are committed to ensuring that [Product Name] meets all the necessary requirements. To that end, we require the following certifications to be completed before we can proceed with the procurement process:

[Certification 1]
[Certification 2]
[Certification 3]
We kindly request that you provide us with a timeline for completing these certifications as soon as possible. We are committed to working closely with you to ensure that the certification process is as smooth and efficient as possible. Please let us know if you require any additional information or support from our team.

By ensuring that [Product Name] meets all the necessary certification requirements, we can improve our vendor relationships and streamline the procurement process. We greatly appreciate your attention to this matter and look forward to continuing to work with you to bring [Product Name] to market.

Thank you for your cooperation.

Best regards,

RAHUL PARMAR

[Your Name]

EMAIL 104: ANALYZING MARKET TRENDS FOR INCREASED PRODUCT SALES

Analyzing market trends can be a game-changer for software project managers looking to increase product sales and revenue. By keeping a finger on the pulse of the market, project managers can identify emerging opportunities, potential pitfalls, and customer needs that may have otherwise gone unnoticed. Analyzing market trends can also help project managers to refine their messaging and promotional materials to better resonate with the target audience. Ultimately, by incorporating market insights into their projects, software project managers can position their products for greater success and achieve their sales goals more effectively.

Sample Email:

Subject Line: Product Market Analysis for [Product Name]

Dear [Sales Team],

I hope this email finds you well. As we move forward with the development of [Product Name], I wanted to take a moment to share some important insights that I have gathered through the product market analysis.

The analysis has revealed some key market trends that we should keep in mind as we develop and market [Product Name]. Specifically, there is a growing demand for products in the [specific market niche] that [Product Name] is uniquely positioned to address. Additionally, there are some gaps in the current market offerings that we can leverage to differentiate ourselves from the competition.

In order to capitalize on these opportunities, we will need to ensure that our marketing and sales efforts are aligned with the needs and preferences of the target market. This may require some adjustments to our messaging and promotional materials, as well as a deeper understanding of the target customers' pain points and decision-making criteria.

I am confident that by staying attuned to the market trends and leveraging our unique product offering, we can increase product sales and revenue. I encourage you to take some time to review the market analysis and incorporate its insights into your sales strategy.

Please let me know if you have any questions or concerns regarding the product market analysis or its implications for our sales strategy. I am here to support you in any way that I can.

Thank you for your hard work and dedication to the success of [Product Name]. I look forward to working with you to achieve our goals.

Best regards,

EMAIL 105: TECHNICAL DEBT MANAGEMENT FOR SUCCESSFUL SOFTWARE DEVELOPMENT

Technical debt can accrue in a software project when a developer takes a shortcut or skips a task to meet deadlines, which can create problems later. To ensure successful software development, technical debt management is crucial. By having a technical debt management plan in place, software project managers can identify and manage technical debt effectively, reduce the risk of future issues, and improve development efficiency and product quality. This approach involves identifying high technical debt areas, prioritizing them, allocating resources, creating a backlog, and incorporating technical debt items into sprint planning. By staying on top of technical debt, software project managers can achieve successful software development and create high-quality products that meet customer needs.

Sample Email:

Subject Line: Project Technical Debt Management Plan for [Project Name]

Dear [Developer Name],

I hope you're doing well. As we're progressing towards the development of [Project Name], I wanted to discuss the technical debt management plan for the project. It's crucial for us to identify, manage, and pay off technical debt, which could affect our project's success if not managed properly.

We all know that technical debt can be a hindrance to development, affecting development efficiency and product quality. Technical debt is a situation where some code is intentionally or unintentionally skipped to meet deadlines, but it could lead to problems in the future. Therefore, it's vital that we plan and manage technical debt from the beginning.

To manage technical debt effectively, we must start by identifying the areas where the technical debt is high, prioritize the technical debt areas, and allocate resources accordingly to address these areas. This will help us reduce the debt while not affecting the development timelines.

To pay off the technical debt, we must regularly set aside time to address the identified areas. I believe we should create a backlog of technical debt items and incorporate them into our sprint planning. By doing this, we will ensure that the technical debt is always a part of our development efforts.

Overall, our technical debt management plan will help us improve our development efficiency and product quality. It's essential that we stay on top of our technical debt, and I'm confident that we can achieve this together.

Please let me know if you have any questions or concerns regarding the technical debt management plan. I would be more than happy to discuss this with you further.

Thank you for your hard work and dedication to this project. I look forward to working with you to make [Project Name] a success.

Best regards,
[Your Name]

EMAIL 106: CHANGE IMPACT ANALYSIS REQUEST FOR PROJECT SUCCESS

A change impact analysis provides project managers with the tools they need to make informed decisions about proposed changes. It helps to identify potential risks and minimize their impact on the project timeline, budget, and resources. This analysis also promotes transparent communication about the impact of changes, building trust and confidence among stakeholders. Ultimately, proactively managing change through a change impact analysis can lead to improved project success rates, stakeholder satisfaction, and a higher likelihood of achieving project goals.

Sample Email:

Subject Line: Project Change Impact Analysis for [Project Name]

Dear [Functional Manager Name],

I hope this email finds you well. I wanted to take a moment to discuss the importance of conducting a change impact analysis for [Project Name]. As we all know, changes are an inevitable part of any project, but without proper analysis, they can lead to delays, budget overruns, and even project failure.

By conducting a change impact analysis, we can identify the potential impact of any proposed changes on the project timeline, budget, and resources. This analysis will help us make informed decisions about whether to proceed with the changes or to explore alternative solutions. It will also ensure that we are proactively managing any potential risks and minimizing the impact on the project and stakeholders.

In addition to its risk management benefits, a change impact analysis can also help to improve project success rates and stakeholder satisfaction. By providing clear and transparent communication about the impact of changes, we can build trust and confidence among stakeholders and demonstrate our commitment to delivering a high-quality project.

I would like to request your support in conducting a change impact analysis for any proposed changes to [Project Name]. I believe that this analysis will greatly benefit the project and ensure its success. Please let me know if you have any questions or concerns regarding this request, and I would be more than happy to discuss it with you further.

Thank you for your support and collaboration on this project. I look forward to continuing to work with you to ensure its success.

Best regards,
[Your Name]

EMAIL 107: PROJECT PERFORMANCE IMPROVEMENT PLAN

In any organization, project performance is critical to achieving success. However, identifying areas for improvement and creating an effective plan can be challenging. The value of creating a project performance improvement plan is significant as it enables software project managers to identify specific actions that can be taken to improve project metrics and increase stakeholder satisfaction. By creating a plan that includes a timeline for implementing improvements and metrics for tracking progress, project managers can ensure that their projects are successful and deliver value to the organization. A well-executed project performance improvement plan can lead to increased efficiency, higher quality deliverables, and ultimately, improved project success rates. So, if you're a software project manager looking to improve your project performance, creating a project performance improvement plan is a critical step towards achieving success.

Sample Email:

Subject Line: Project Performance Improvement Plan for [Project Name]

Dear [Boss Name],

I hope this email finds you well. As the software project manager for [Project Name], I wanted to take a moment to provide you with an update on our project performance and share with you a plan for improvement.

After reviewing the project metrics and stakeholder feedback, I have identified several areas where we can improve project performance. Specifically, I believe we can increase development efficiency by improving our project management practices and optimizing our resource allocation. Additionally, we can enhance the quality of our deliverables by implementing stricter quality control measures and introducing more frequent code reviews.

I understand that improving project performance is a top priority for our organization and that the success of this project is critical to our long-term success. Therefore, I have created a detailed project performance improvement plan that outlines the specific actions we will take to improve our project metrics and achieve our goals.

This plan includes a timeline for implementing the identified improvements, as well as metrics for tracking our progress and measuring our success. I am confident that by following this plan, we can improve our project success rates and increase stakeholder satisfaction.

I have attached the project performance improvement plan to this email for your review. Please let me know if you have any questions or concerns regarding the plan or if you require any additional information.

Thank you for your continued support and trust in my ability to lead this project to success.

Best regards,
[Your Name]

EMAIL 108: ENSURING PRODUCT ROADMAP ALIGNMENT WITH VENDORS

As a software project manager, it's crucial to maintain strong relationships with vendors and ensure that our product roadmaps align. Doing so can provide numerous benefits, such as improved product quality, streamlined development processes, and increased customer satisfaction. By communicating regularly with vendors and addressing any potential misalignments, software project managers can ensure that their projects remain on track and that all stakeholders are working towards the same goals. By utilizing the email template provided, project managers can easily check in with vendors and make any necessary adjustments, ultimately leading to more successful projects and partnerships.

Sample Email:

Subject Line: Product Roadmap Alignment Check-In for [Product Name]

Dear [Vendor Contact Name],

I hope this email finds you well. As the software project manager for [Product Name], I wanted to check in with you regarding the alignment of our product roadmaps.

As we continue to develop and improve [Product Name], it's essential that our goals and plans align with those of our valued vendors. This ensures that we can work together effectively to bring the best possible product to market.

I wanted to take this opportunity to discuss any potential misalignments that may have occurred and work with you to correct them. By doing so, we can ensure that our partnership remains strong, and we can continue to provide high-quality products to our customers.

Please let me know if there are any changes or updates to your roadmap that we should be aware of. Additionally, if you have any concerns or feedback about our roadmap, I would be more than happy to discuss this with you.

Thank you for your continued partnership and support. I look forward to working with you to ensure the success of [Product Name].

Best regards,
[Your Name]

EMAIL 109: BOOSTING SALES THROUGH EFFECTIVE PRODUCT PROMOTION

A well-planned and executed product promotion can have a significant impact on your sales and revenue. By utilizing a mix of traditional and digital marketing techniques, you can increase your product's visibility and engage with customers in new and exciting ways. This can not only drive immediate sales but also establish long-term brand loyalty and customer relationships.

But effective product promotion requires careful planning and execution. As a software project manager, you can play a critical role in this process by providing support and guidance to your sales team. By collaborating with them, you can ensure that your product promotion plan is well-informed, well-executed, and aligns with the overall goals of your organization.

Sample Email:

Subject Line: Product Promotion Plan for [Product Name]

Dear [Sales Team],

I hope this email finds you well. I wanted to reach out to you today to discuss our product promotion plan for [Product Name]. As we all know, promotions are a critical component of increasing product sales and revenue, and I believe that we can greatly improve our approach to them.

After conducting some research and analysis, I have developed a detailed promotion plan that I believe will help us achieve our sales goals. The plan includes a mix of both digital and traditional marketing techniques, such as email marketing, social media advertising, print ads, and promotional events.

To ensure that the plan is successful, I will be working closely with you to provide support and guidance throughout the promotion period. I encourage you to be creative and think outside the box when it comes to promoting our product. The more unique and engaging our promotions are, the more likely they are to be successful.

I understand that promotions can be a significant investment of time and resources, but I strongly believe that the potential benefits far outweigh the costs. By increasing our product sales and revenue, we can ensure the long-term success of our company and continue to provide value to our customers.

Please let me know if you have any questions or concerns regarding the promotion plan. I am happy to discuss this with you further and provide any additional support that you may need.

Thank you for your hard work and dedication to promoting our product. I look forward to working with you to achieve our sales goals.

RAHUL PARMAR

Best regards,
[Your Name]

EMAIL 110: CONQUERING COMMUNICATION CHALLENGES: KEY TAKEAWAYS AND ENCOURAGEMENT FOR SUCCESS

Effective communication is the cornerstone of success in software project management. Whether you are communicating with team members, clients, or stakeholders, the way you communicate can have a significant impact on the outcome of your project. In this book, we have provided 100 email templates for every scenario that a software project manager could face, along with tips for customizing those templates to suit different situations.

The key takeaway from this book is that effective communication is about more than just having the right words to say. It is about understanding your audience, adjusting your tone and language, and customizing your message to suit the situation. By using the templates and customization tips provided in this book, software project managers can improve their communication skills and achieve better outcomes for their projects.

We have covered some best practices for effective email communication, including keeping it clear and concise, using the right tone, being mindful of timing, and using descriptive subject lines. We have also highlighted some common pitfalls to avoid in project communication, such as rambling emails, negativity, spelling and grammar errors, and vague requests.

Customizing your email templates is equally important for effective communication. We have provided tips for customizing the tone, personalizing the content, using the right language, and tailoring the format to suit different situations. By following these tips, software project managers can improve their communication skills and build stronger relationships with their team members, clients, and stakeholders.

In conclusion, effective communication is critical to the success of any software project, and email is a key component of that communication. By using the templates and customization tips provided in this book, software project managers can streamline their communication process, save time, and achieve better outcomes for their projects. We encourage readers to provide feedback and ask questions about the templates provided, and to continue learning and improving their communication skills. Together, we can conquer communication challenges and achieve success in software project management.

A BIG THANK YOU!

I wanted to take a moment to express my sincere gratitude for choosing "The Ultimate Resource for Software Project Managers: 100 Email Templates for Every Project Scenario" as your go-to resource for effective communication and project management.

As a software project manager myself, I know firsthand the challenges that come with effective communication in the workplace. That's why I am thrilled that our email templates have helped you save time, streamline your workflow, and achieve your project goals more effectively.

Creating this book was a labor of love for us. Our team of experts worked tirelessly to provide you with a comprehensive collection of expertly crafted email templates that can be used in any project scenario. Our goal was to make communication easier and more efficient, allowing you to focus on delivering high-quality projects on time and within budget.

We firmly believe that the 100+ email templates provided in this book are among the best available for software project managers, and we are confident that they will help you achieve success in your projects. But don't just take our word for it - we encourage you to try out these templates for yourself and see the results firsthand.

Your feedback is incredibly important to us. We would be grateful if you could take a few moments to leave a review and share your experience with other software project managers. Your feedback will help us continue to provide high-quality resources to professionals like you.

Once again, thank you for choosing "The Ultimate Resource for Software Project Managers: 100 Email Templates for Every Project Scenario." We wish you the best of luck in your future projects, and we hope that this book has helped you achieve success and streamline your workflow.

If you have any feedback or comments, please do not hesitate to reach out to us at emailbox24by7@gmail.com